A COURSE IN HINDI

HINDI TEXT BOOK

VANI PRAKASHAN

21-A, Daryaganj, New Delhi-110002 (India)
Phone : 91-011-23275710, 23273167, 51562622
Mobile : 9811053214 Fax : 91-011-23275710
e-mail : vani_prakashan@yahoo.com
vani_prakashan@mantraonline.com

A Course In Hindi

Dr. P. Jayaraman

VANI PRAKASHAN

VANI PRAKASHAN
ज्ञान के विविध आयामों के प्रकाशक

Vani Prakashan's logo is a creation of the strokes from the
paintbrush of the veteran artist M.F. Husain
Vani Prakashan, 21-A, Daryaganj New Delhi-110002

A COURSE IN HINDI

by Dr. P. Jayaraman

Hindi-English Grammar Teaching

ISBN : 978-8143-340-8

2005 Ist Edition

2010 : Edition
Price : In India Rs. 300/-

In USA $ 25

VANI PRAKASHAN
Phone : 0091#11#23273167, 23275710
Fax : 0091#11#23275710
website : www.vaniprakashan.in
E-mail : vaniprakashan@gmail.com
vani_prakashan@yahoo.com

Printed by : Mehara Offset Press, Delhi-110002

Preface

Hindi, the national and official language of India, is spoken and understood by the large majority of Indians in India and abroad. Hindi is also taught in schools in many Indian states as well. As a language—a medium of communication, Hindi has taken the first position among all the Indian languages. Among the elite, in the business community and in public sector companies and corporations, as well as in the Government offices, Hindi is commonly used along with English.

During my twenty-five years of teaching Hindi in the USA, I have found a keen interest both in the Indian and the non-Indian communities to learn Hindi as a language for variety of reasons ranging from an interest in India, her culture, philosophy and people, and a desire to travel across the country and communicate with the local people there in their own language, to the influence of Bollywood movies, Hindi music, devotional songs, ghazals, etc.

People in general want to speak and understand the language more than to read and write. I, therefore, started teaching Hindi first in Roman script, concentrating on the spoken aspect of the language and gradually introducing the students to the Hindi script known as Nagari or Devanagari script. The lessons are therefore prepared in both scripts - Roman and Devanagari to enable the students to speak the language first and then slowly to learn to read and write. My main endeavor is to make students feel comfortable to communicate in Hindi as well as to make them understand the language. This was possible in three sessions spread over a total of thirty classes. A concommitant objective was to make students understand and speak grammatically correct Hindi. The lessons are prepared keeping in mind the above objective. In each lesson students are taught the language commonly spoken by Hindi speaking people with an emphasis on the elements of grammar introduced through exercise / questions-answers (on some occasions, grammar rules are also explained in a simple language).

We should keep in mind that this book is meant for those who are non-Hindi speaking and who do not have any knowledge of Hindi and wish to learn the language from scratch. A few sentence constructions are peculiar to Hindi such as the use of 'ne' in the past tense, 'chaahiye', 'lag', 'sak', 'chuk' and post-positions; I have therefore introduced the peculiarities of such usages as easily as possible in many of these lessons.

A few points indicated below are required to be noted before starting to learn Hindi.

1. Nouns in Hindi are either masculine or feminine in gender. One can know the gender of nouns only by learning the gender along with each noun. A few rules can be given. The words ending with 'aa' are generally masculine and 'ee' feminine. But the gender of a noun should be memorized along with the noun.

2. Construction of sentences in Hindi is not like that in English. The subject comes first and the verb (preceded by any object) comes at the end of the sentence (all Indian languages have the same character).

3. There are no definite or indefinite articles (a, an, the) in Hindi.

4. What we have as prepositions in English, are post-positions in Hindi since they are used <u>after</u> the noun or pronoun.

5. Hindi has 13 vowels and 33 consonants. These will be taught gradually in the first session of the course. A peculiarity of Hindi is aspirated consonants (see below).

Words are presented in Roman script as they are pronounced. For example

वह instead of writing this as VAH, we have given its spoken form VO on the English side; यह instead of writing this as YAH, we have given its spoken form YE(h) but here 'h' (ह) is silent.

The sounds of ड़ (ḍa), ढ़ (ḍha), द (da/tha), ध (dha), श (ṣa), ष (sha) and स (sa) should be taught by the teacher clearly.

ङ, ञ, ण, न are given in English as 'n' but they have their specific nasal sounds which should also be taught by the teacher. There are also half nasal sounds which are indicated by a symbol — on the top of the letter, such as में, मैं, हूं, हैं, etc. While writing them in Roman Script, we have used (n) in parenthesis, such as Me(n), My(n), Hoo(n), Hai(n), etc.

6. I have not given rules for the pronunciation of Hindi words as I feel that they should be taught by teachers in the classroom.

It has been my experience that if a student meticulously follows the classroom teaching and spares time to study by himself or herself, he or she will be able to speak, read and write the language competently and effortlessly in a short time.

I hope, the students will find this book useful and that teachers will also accept this book as a reference book to support their skill to make the student feel at home in learning the language.

I would welcome suggestions from teachers for improving the quality and usefulness of the book.

Before concluding, I wish to thank and express my gratitude towards Shri Arun Maheshwari, Vani Prakashan, New Delhi for publishing this book in record time. It was only his perseverance that made me collect my lessons and put them in order.

My thanks are also due to Dr. Suresh Kumar who meticulously went through the script and offered many important suggestions to improve the quality of the book.

Hundreds of students have been sources of inspiration for me; however, I would like to give credit to one special student - Kalpana (Esther T. Loewengart) who not only inspired my enthusiasm but also offered valuable suggestions to make this book useful. My special thanks to her as well as to all my students.

New York   **Dr. P. Jayaraman**
February 15, 2005

Contents

Part I

Hindi Course For Beginners

Session I

10 Lessons

Hindi Script
(Known as Nagari or Devanagari Script)

Vowels 13

अ	A/a	आ	AA/aa
इ	I/i	ई	EE/ee
उ	U/u	ऊ	OO/oo
		ऋ	R/ṛ
ए	E/e	ऐ	AY/AI or ay/ai
ओ	O/o	औ	AU/au
अं	AM/ am	अः	AH*/ ah*

* not in much use

Lesson I

Namaste/Namaskar	A word for greeting

1. **Read and learn the following sentences :**

TUMHARAA NAAM KYA HAI ? *(informal)*	What is your name?
AAPKAA NAAM KYAA HAI? *(formal)*	What is your name ?
MERAA NAAM JOSEPH HAI.	My name is Joseph
MERAA NAAM ANITA HAI.	My name is Anita
*YE(h) KALAM HAI.	This is a pen
YE(h) KITAAB HAI	This is a book
YE(h) GHAR HAI	This is a house
YE(h) KAMRAA HAI.	This is a room.
*VO BILLE HAI.	That is a cat
VO KUTHTHAA HAI	That is a dog
VO PAANEE HAI.	That is water
VO DOODH HAI	That is milk
YE(h) MERAA GHAR HAI	This is my house
VO TUMHARAA/AAPKAA GHAR HAI	That is your house
YE(h) MERAA BHAAYEE HAI	This is my brother.
VO MEREE BEHAN HAI	She is my sister.

---

*   'VAH' is written is Hindi, but pronounced as 'VO'

       'YAH' is written in Hindi, but pronounced as 'Ye(h)'

       (The general rule is : When 'H' is used at the end of a word, it is silent; not pronounced)

पाठ 1

नमस्ते/नमस्कार

I तुम्हारा नाम क्या है?
आपका नाम क्या है?
मेरा नाम जोसफ़ है।
मेरा नाम अनीता है।
यह कलम है।
यह किताब है।
यह घर है।
यह कमरा है।
वह बिल्ली है।
वह कुत्ता है।
वह पानी है।
वह दूध है।
यह मेरा घर है।
वह तुम्हारा/आपका घर है
यह मेरा भाई है।
वह मेरी बहन है।

II. Learn the following :

Pronouns

Singular		Plural	
I am	MY(n) HOO(n)	We are	†HUM HAI(n) / HUM LOG HAI(n)
You are	TUM HO	You are	TUM LOG HO **informal**
You are	AAP HAI(n)	You are	AAP LOG HAI(n) **formal**
He is	VO HAI	They are	VE HAI(n)
She is		Those are	
It is			
This is	YE(h) HAI	These are	YE HAI(n)
Who is	KAUN HAI	Who are	KAUN HAI(n)

III. New words :

Kitaab*	book	Kalam*	Pen	Naam	Name
Ladkaa Boy	Ladkee* Girl	Ghar	House/home	Kamraa	Room
Paanee	Water	Doodh	Milk	Bhaayee	Brother
Behan*	Sister	Billee*	Cat	Kuththaa	Dog
Kaun	Who	Kyaa	What	Kahaa(n)	Where
Vahaa(n)	There	Yahaa(n)	Here		

IV. Read :

Ye(h) kaun hai	Who is this?
Ye(h) ladkaa hai	This is a boy
Ye(h) ladkee hai	This is a girl
Vahaa(n) kaun hai?	Who is there?
Vahaa(n) mera bhaayee hai	There is my brother.
Vahaa(n) kyaa hai?	What is there?
Vahaa(n) mera ghar hai	There is my house.
Vahaa(n) mera school hai	There is my school.

Vo kaun hai?	Who is that?
Vo ladka hai	He is a boy
Vo ladkee hai	She is a girl

---

†   HUM = We, It is generally used for two people and even for many but to specify the plurality, HUM LOG is used.

*   Indicates feminine words.

II

मैं हूं	हम हैं/हम लोग हैं
तुम हो	तुम लोग हो
आप हैं	आप लोग हैं
वह है	वे हैं
यह है	ये हैं
कौन है	कौन हैं

III

किताब	कलम	नाम	लड़का	लड़की
घर	कमरा	पानी	दूध	
भाई	बहन	बिल्ली	कुत्ता	
कौन	क्या	कहां	वहां	यहां

IV

यह कौन है?	वह कौन है?
यह लड़का है।	वह लड़का है।
यह लड़की है।	वह लड़की है।
वहां कौन है?	
वहां मेरा भाई है।	
वहां क्या है?	
वहां मेरा घर है।	
वहां मेरा स्कूल है	

Lesson 2

I. Shabd (words) :

Nouns :

Aadmee	man	Aurat*	woman	Bachchaa	child (male)	Ghodaa	horse
Chaai*	tea	Zameen*	floor	Bachchee*	child (female)	Rotee*	bread
Mez	table	Kursee*	chair	Haath	hand	Sabak	lesson
Kelaa	banana	Chaaval	rice				

Verbs :

Utt	get up	Bytt	sit	Padh	read	Likh	write
Khaa	eat	Laa	bring	Gaa	Sing	Khel	play
So	sleep	Kar	do	Pee	drink	De	give
Le	take						

†Adjectives :

Achchhaa	good	Buraa	Bad	Chotaa	small
Badaa	big	Tandaa	cold	Garam	hot
Meettaa	sweet	Khattaa	sour		

**Pre-positions :

Me(n)	in	Par	on	Se	from / by / with

---

†   See page 30 for explanation

**   Pre-positions are used after nouns or pronouns in Hindi; hence called post-positions.

पाठ 2

I   शब्द :

आदमी	औरत	बच्चा	घोड़ा
चाय	ज़मीन	बच्ची	रोटी
मेज़	कुरसी	हाथ	सबक
केला	चावल		

उठ	बैठ	पढ़	लिख
खा	ला	गा	खेल
सो	कर	पी	दे
ले			

अच्छा	बुरा	छोटा
बड़ा	ठंडा	गरम
मीठा	खट्टा	

में	पर	से

II. Read these sentences (Imperative) :

Informal

A.

TUM YAHAA(n) AAO,	(You) come here.
TUM VAHAA(n) JAAO	(You) go there
TUM KURSEE PAR BYTTO	(You) sit on the chair.
TUM ZAMEEN PAR MAT BYTTO	(You) **don't sit** on the floor.
TUM CHAAVAL KHAAO	(You) eat rice.
TUM ROTEE BHEE KHAAO.	(You) also eat bread. (bhee = also)
TUM ACHCHHAA KAAM KARO	(You) do good work.
TUM KALAM LAAO	(You) bring a pen.
TUM GHAR ME(n) SO'O	(You) sleep in the house.
TUM TANDAA PAANEE PIO	(You) drink cold water.
TUM GARAM CHAAI PIO	(You) drink hot tea.
TUM TANDEE CHAAI MAT PIO	(You) **don't drink** cold tea.
TUM KALAM LO	(You) take a pen.
TUM KITAAB DO	(You) give a book.

Notes :

1. Imperative mood of the verb is formed by adding ओ (O) to the verb root when the subject is तुम (Tum). Respect/plural is expressed by adding इये (iye) to the verb root –

   तुम आओ (Tum bytto) (you) come
   तुम बैठो (Tum baitto) (you) sit
   आप आइये (Aap aaiye) ⎫ (Please) come ⎫ In respect
   आप बैठिये (Aap byttiye) ⎬ (Please) sit. ⎬ Plural
   आप लोग आइये (Aap log aaiye) ⎪
   आप लोग बैठिये (Aap log byttiye) ⎭

2. The following verbs are exceptions to the above. In respect/plural जिये (jiye) is added to the verb root.

   पी - पीजिये   दे - दीजिये
   (Pee - Peejiye)   (De - Deejiye)
   Please drink   Please give

II Read these Sentences (Imperative) :

Informal

A तुम यहां आओ

तुम वहां जाओ।

तुम कुरसी पर बैठो।

तुम ज़मीन पर मत बैठो।

तुम चावल खाओ।

तुम रोटी भी खाओ

तुम अच्छा काम करो।

तुम कलम लाओ।

तुम घर में सोओ।

तुम ठंडा पानी पिओ।

तुम गरम चाय पिओ।

तुम ठंडी चाय मत पिओ।

तुम कलम लो।

तुम किताब दो।

ले - लीजिये	कर - कीजिये
(Le - Leejiye)	(Kar - Keejiye)
Please take	Please do

3. To express the negative मत (Mat) is used before the imperative form of the verb.

मत आओ	मत बैठो
Mat Aao	Mat Bytto
Don't come	Don't sit
मत आइये	मत बैठिये
Mat Aaiye	Mat Byttiye
Please don't come.	Please don't sit.

4. When ओ (O) is added to verb roots दे (De) and ले (Le) they become दो (Do) and लो (Lo)

Formal

B. AAP GHAR AAIYE — Please come home.

AAP VAHAA(n) JAAIYE — Please go there.

AAP KURSEE PAR BYTTIYE — Please sit on the chair.

AAP ZAMEEN PAR MAT BYTTIYE — Please don't sit on the floor.

AAP CHAAI PEEJIYE — Please drink tea.

AAP TANDAA PAANEE DEEJIYE — Please give cold water.

AAP ACHCHAA KAAM KEEJIYE — Please do good work.

AAP COFFEE LEEJIYE — Please take coffee.

C. Haath **me(n)** kyaa hai? — Mez **par** kitaab hai.
What is **in** hand? — A book is **on** the table.

Haath **me(n)** kalam hai. — Mez **par** kalam bhee hai — Ghar **me(n)** billee hai
A pen is in hand — A pen is also on the table — A cat is in the house

Tum kalam **se** likho — (You) write with pen.
Tum bus **se** jaao — (You) go **by** bus.
Tum ghar **se** aao. — (You) come **from** home.

Formal

B   आप घर आइये।
    आप वहां जाइये।
    आप कुरसी पर बैठिये।
    आप ज़मीन पर मत बैठिये।
    आप चाय पीजिये।
    आप ठंडा पानी दीजिये।
    आप अच्छा काम कीजिये।
    आप काफ़ी लीजिये।

C   हाथ **में** क्या है?   मेज़ **पर** किताब है।
    हाथ **में** कलम है।   मेज़ **पर** कलम भी है।

    तुम कलम **से** लिखो।   घर **में** बिल्ली है।
    तुम बस **से** जाओ।
    तुम घर **से** आओ।

Consonants 33(+A)

Velar	क	ख	ग	घ	ङ *
	Ka	Kha	Ga	Gha	n
Palatal	च	छ	ज	झ	ञ *
	Cha	Chha	Ja	Jha	n
Retroflex	ट	ठ	ड	ढ	ण
	Ta	Tta	Da	Dha	**ṇa**
Dental	त	थ	द	ध	न
	Tha	Tha	Da	Dha	Na
Bilabial	प	फ	ब	भ	म
	Pa	Pha	Ba	Bha	Ma

य	र	ल	व
Ya	Ra	La	Va
श	ष	स	ह
Ṣa	Sha	Sa	Ha
ज़	फ़	ड़	ढ़
Za	Fa	Ḍa	Ḍha

---

* **Note** : ङ (n) ञ (n) are not used in modern Hindi; Instead ं is used to denote the sound
For example :

    आंख (Aaṇkh)
    पांच (Paaṇch)

Lesson 3

1. Shabd (Words) :

Masculine Nouns (Singular & Plural)

Laḍkaa	boy	Laḍke	boys	Bachchaa	child	Bachche	children
Kamraa	room	Kamre	rooms	Ghoḍaa	horse	Ghoḍe	horses
Kuththaa	dog	Kuththe	dogs	Kelaa	banana	Kele	bananas

Feminine Nouns (Singular & Plural)

Laḍkee	girl	Laḍkiyaa(n)	girls	Bachchee	child	Bachchiyaa(n)	children
Billee	cat	Billiyaa(n)	cats	Kursee	chair	Kursiyaan(n)	chairs
Kitaab	book	Kitaabe(n)	books	Saḍak	road	Saḍke(n)	roads
Behan	sister	Behne(n)	sisters	Aankh	eye	Aankhe(n)	eyes

Nouns ending with other vowels or consonants (masculine/feminine) will mostly remain unchanged in plural.

Some More Nouns :

Peḍ	tree	Paudha	plant	Phool	flower	Phal	fruit
Paththaa	leaf	Paththee (f)	small leaf	Anaar	pomegranate	Angoor	grape
Amrood	guava	Aam	mango	Santraa	orange	Seb	apple
Khajoor	date (fruit)						

II Learn the following sentences :

(A) Kursee zameen par hai. Mez bhee zameen par hai.

Kursee aur mez zameen par hai(n)

Bachchaa ghar me(n) hai. Bachche ghar me(n) hai(n)

पाठ 3

I शब्द :

Masculins Nouns (Singular & Plural)

लड़का	लड़के	बच्चा	बच्चे
कमरा	कमरे	घोड़ा	घोड़े
कुता	कुत्ते	केला	केले

Feminine Nouns (Singular & Plural)

लड़की	लड़कियां	बच्ची	बच्चियां
बिल्ली	बिल्लियां	कुर्सी	कुरसियां
किताब	किताबें	सड़क	सड़कें
बहन	बहनें	आंख	आंखें

Some more Nouns :

पेड़	पौधा	फूल	फल
पत्ता	पत्ती	अनार	अंगूर
अमरूद	आम	संतरा	सेब
खजूर			

II Learn the following sentences :

अ) कुर्सी ज़मीन पर है।   मेज़ भी ज़मीन पर है।

कुर्सी और मेज़ ज़मीन पर हैं।

बच्चा घर में है।   बच्चे घर में हैं।

Bachchiyaa(n) bhee ghar
    me(n) hai(n).
Bachche aur bachchiyaa(n)
    ghar me(n) hai(n).
Ye(h) meraa kamraa hai
Tumharaa kamraa kahaa(n) hai?   Meraa kamraa vahaa(n) hai.

Vo meraa bhaayee hai.   Vo meree behan hai.
Tumhaaree behne(n)
    kahaa(n) hai(n)?   Meree behne(n) school me(n) hai(n).
Meree maa(n) ghar me(n) hai.   Mere pitaa ji bhee ghar me(n) hai(n).
Haath me(n) kyaa hai?   Haath me(n) kalam hai.
Kalam me(n) **syaahee** hai.
    (syaahee = ink)
Aapki kalam kahaa(n) hai?   Meree kalam mez par hai.
Meree kalam aur kitaab mez par hai (n)

(B) Paanee tandaa hai.   Chaai garam hai.
Paanee garam nahee(n) hai.   Chaai tandee nahee(n) hai
Vo ladkaa achchhaa hai.   Vo ladkee achchhee hai.
Ve ladke achchhe hai(n)   Ve ladkiyaa(n) achchhee hai(n)
Meraa kamraa chhotaa hai.   Meraa ghar chhotaa nahee(n) hai.

(C) Tum ghar aao.   Tum vahaa(n) mat jaao.
Tum kursee par bytto.   Tum zameen par mat bytto.

Note : Bhee = also; Aur = and; Nahee(n) = not; it is used before the verb.

बच्चियां भी घर में हैं।

बच्चे और बच्चियां घर में हैं।

यह मेरा कमरा है।

तुम्हारा कमरा कहां है? मेरा कमरा वहां है।

वह मेरा भाई है। वह मेरी बहन है।

तुम्हारी बहनें कहां हैं? मेरी बहनें स्कूल में हैं।

मेरी मां घर में है। मेरे पिताजी भी घर में हैं।

हाथ में क्या है? हाथ में कलम है।

कलम में **स्याही** है

आपकी कलम कहां है? मेरी कलम मेज़ पर है।

मेरी कलम और किताब मेज़ पर हैं।

आ) पानी ठंडा है। चाय गरम है।

पानी गरम नहीं है। चाय ठंडी नहीं है।

वह लड़का अच्छा है। वह लड़की अच्छी है।

वे लड़के अच्छे हैं। वे लड़कियां अच्छी हैं।

मेरा कमरा छोटा है। मेरा घर छोटा नहीं है।

इ) तुम घर आओ। तुम वहां मत जाओ।

तुम कुरसी पर बैठो। तुम ज़मीन पर मत बैठो।

Tum kalam se likho   Tum bus se ghar jaao.

Tum chaai pio.   Tum kalam do. (give)   DE is the root verb.

Aap ghar aaiye.   Aap vahaa(n) mat jaaiye.   Aap kitaab padhiye.

Aap paanee peejiye.   Aap kalam deejiye.

Aap kalam leejiye.   Aap kaam keejiye.

Combination of Consonants and Vowels

Vowels	Vowel symbols to be added to the consonants	Consonants			
अ	—	क	ka	च	Cha
आ	ा	का	kaa	चा	Chaa
इ	ि	कि	ki	चि	Chi
ई	ी	की	kee	ची	Chee
उ	ु	कु	ku	चु	Chu
ऊ	ू	कू	koo	चू	Choo
ऋ	ृ	कृ	kr	चृ	Chr
ए	े	के	ke	चे	Che
ऐ	ै	कै	kai	चै	Chai
ओ	ो	को	ko	चो	Cho
औ	ौ	कौ	kau	चौ	Chau
अं	ं	कं	kam	चं	Cham
** अः	ः	कः	kah	चः	Chah

---

* **Note:** Use of Adjectives:

a. An adjective precedes the noun it qualifies.

Achchhaa	Ladkaa	Tandaa	Paanee
good	boy	cold	water

तुम कलम से लिखो।   तुम बस से घर जाओ।
तुम चाय पिओ।   तुम कलम दो।

आप घर आइये।   आप वहां मत जाइये।   आप किताब पढ़िये।
आप पानी पीजिये   आप कलम दीजिये।
आप कलम लीजिये।   आप काम कीजिये।

---

b. Adjectives ending with 'aa' will change to 'e' when they qualify a masculine plural noun and to 'ee' when they qualify a feminine singular or plural noun.

1. Achchhaa Laḍkaa   Achchhe Laḍke
    Achchhee Laḍkee   Achchhee Laḍkiyaa(n)
2. Chotaa bachchaa   Chote bachche
    Chotee bachchee   Chotee bachchiyaa(n)

Adjective not ending with 'aa' will not change. They will remain the same :

Garam Paanee   Garam Chaai

** Not in much use

Lesson 4

1. Shabd (Words) :

Nouns

Ghar	House/Home	Makaan	Building	Chath*	Roof
Khiḍkee*	Window	Darvaazaa	Door	Daree*	Carpet
Deevaar*	Wall	Ghaḍee*	Clock	Tasveer*	Picture
Seedheee*	Staircase/Stairs/Ladder	Bageechaa	Garden	Pankhaa	Fan

Sabzee*	Vegetable	Tamaatar	Tomato	Byngan	Eggplant
Gaajar	Carrot	Bhindee*	Okra	Sahjan	Drumstick
Aaloo	Potato	Pyaaj	Onion	Lahsun	Garlic
Gobhee*	Cabbage	Phool Gobhee*	Cauliflower		

Verbs

Khel	play	So	sleep	Jaag	wake up
Ro	cry	Seekh	learn	Sikhaa	teach
Dauḍ	run	Khareed	buy	Bech	sell

II. Sentences (Present Tense) :

To make a verb into present tense, add Thaa (masculine singular) The (masculine plural) Thee (feminine singular & plural) to the verb followed by hoo(n), ho, hai, hai(n) depending upon the subject.

Masculine		Feminine	
My(n) yahaa(n) aathaa hoo(n)	I come here	My(n) yahaa(n) aathee hoo(n)	I come here
My(n) ghar jaathaa hoo(n)	I go home	My(n) ghar jaathee hoo(n)	I go home
My(n) rotee khaathaa hoo(n)	I eat bread	My(n) rotee khaathee hoo(n)	I eat bread
My(n) doodh peethaa hoo(n)	I drink milk	My(n) doodh peethee hoo(n)	I drink milk

पाठ-4

I   शब्द :

Nouns

घर	मकान	छत
खिड़की	दरवाज़ा	दरी
दीवार	घड़ी	तसवीर
सीढ़ी	बग़ीचा	पंखा
सब्ज़ी	टमाटर	बैंगन
गाजर	भिंडी	सहजन
आलू	प्याज	लहसुन
गोभी	फूल गोभी	

Verbs

खेल	सो	जाग
रो	सीख	सिखा
दौड़	खरीद	बेच

II   Sentences (Present Tense) :

Masculine	Feminine
मैं यहां आता हूं	मैं यहां आती हूं
मैं घर जाता हूं	मैं घर जाती हूं
मैं रोटी खाता हूं	मैं रोटी खाती हूं
मैं दूध पीता हूं	मैं दूध पीती हूं

Tum Kyaa karthe ho?	What do you do?	Tum Kyaa karthee ho?	What do you do?
Tum kab sothe ho?	When do you sleep?	Tum kab sothee ho?	When do you sleep?
Kyaa tum garam chaai peethe ho?	Do you drink hot tea?	Kyaa tum garam chaai peethee ho?	
Kyaa tum Hindi bolthe ho?	Do you speak Hindi?	Kyaa tum Hindi bolthee ho?	

Vo school jaathaa hai.	He goes to school.	Vo school Jaathee hai	She goes to school.
Bachchaa sothaa hai	The child sleeps	Bachchee sothee hai	The child sleeps
Ladkaa mydaan me(n) khelthaa hai		Ladkee mydaan me(n) nahee(n) khelthee hai	
The boy plays in the playground		The girl does not play in the playground.	

Hum/Hum Log	We		
Aap/Aap Log	you	Phal laathe hai(n) bring fruit/s	Phal laathee hai(n)
Ve	They/Those	Kitaab padhthe hai(n) read book	Kitaab padhthee hai(n)
Ye	These		

III. Numbers :

1-10	Ek	Do	Teen	Chaar	Paa(n)ch	Chhe	Saath
	Aatt	Nau	Das				
11-20	Gyaarah	Baarah	Terah	Chaudah	Pandrah	Solah	Satrah
	Attaarah	Unness	Bees				

IV. Read the following sentences : (Review)

YE(h) KURSEE HAI	VO MEZ HAI.
MEZ ZAMEEN PAR HAI	KURSEE BHEE ZAMEEN PAR HAI.
MEZ PAR KALAM HAI.	MEZ PAR KITAAB BHEE HAI.
MEZ PAR KALAM AUR KITAAB HAI(n),	
HAATH ME(n) KITAAB HAI.	HAATH ME(n) KALAM BHEE HAI.
HAATH ME(n) KITAAB AUR KALAM HAI(n).	
VO GHAR HAI.	VO NAYAA GHAR HAI.
VO GHAR BADAA HAI.	VO GHAR CHOTTAA NAHEE(n) HAI.

तुम क्या करते हो?   तुम क्या करती हो?

तुम कब सोते हो?   तुम कब सोती हो?

क्या तुम गरम चाय पीते हो?   क्या तुम गरम चाय पीती हो?

क्या तुम हिन्दी बोलते हो?   क्या तुम हिन्दी बोलती हो?

वह स्कूल जाता है।   वह स्कूल जाती है।

बच्चा सोता है।   बच्ची सोती है।

लड़का मैदान में खेलता है   लड़की मैदान में नहीं खेलती है।

हम/हम लोग

आप/आप लोग   फल लाते हैं   फल लाती हैं

वे   किताब पढ़ते हैं   किताब पढ़ती हैं

ये

III Numbers :

1-10	एक	दो	तीन	चार	पांच	छे	सात
	आठ	नौ	दस				
11-20	ग्यारह	बारह	तेरह	चौदह	पन्द्रह	सोलह	सत्रह
	अठारह	उन्नीस	बीस				

IV Read the following Sectences : (Review)

यह कुरसी है।   वह मेज़ है।

मेज़ ज़मीन पर है।   कुरसी भी ज़मीन पर है।

मेज़ पर कलम है।   मेज़ पर किताब भी है।

मेज़ पर कलम और किताब हैं।

हाथ में किताब है।   हाथ में कलम भी है।

हाथ में किताब और कलम हैं।

वह घर है।   वह नया घर है।

वह घर बड़ा है।   वह घर छोटा नहीं है।

VE GHAR BAḌE HAI(n).

VE GHAR CHHOTE NAHEE(n) HAI(n).

GHAR ME(n) BACHCHAA HAI.

GHAR ME(n) CHAAR KAMARE HAI(n).

CHAAI GARAM HAI.

CHAAI TANDEE NAHEE(N) HAI.

KYAA KAAFEE BHEE GARAM HAI?

JEE HAA(n) KAAFEE BHEE GARAM HAI.

KAAFEE TANDEE NAHEE(n) HAI

YE(h) KAPḌAA SAFED HAI.

KYAA KAPḌAA SAAF HAI?

JEE HAA(n), KAPḌAA SAAF HAI.

KYAA KAPḌAA KAALAA HAI?

JEE NAHEE(n), KAPḌAA KAALAA NAHEE(N) HAI.

VO BILLEE HAI.

BILLEE CHOTEE HAI.

BILLEE KAALEE HAI.

KYAA BILLEE SAFED HAI?

JEE NAHEE(n), BILLEE KAALEE HAI.

VAHAA(n) KAUN HAI(n)

VAHAA(n) BACHCHE HAI(n).

VAHAA(n) KITNE BACHCHE HAI(n)?

VAHAA(n) BAHUT BACHCHE HAI(n).

(KITNE = HOW MANY/MUCH)

(BAHUT = Many/much)

KYAA VAHAA(n) BACHCHIYAA(n) BHEE HAI (n)?

JEE HAA(n), VAHAA(n) BACHCHIYAA(n) BHEE HAI(n)

KYAA YE(h) TUMHAARAA GHAR HAI?

JEE HAA(n), YE(h) MERAA GHAR HAI.

KYAA VO BHEE TUMHAARAA GHAR HAI?

JEE NAHEE(n), VO MERAA GHAR NAHEE(n) HAI.

KYAA TUMHAARAA GHAR BAḌAA HAI?

JEE NAHEE(n) MERAA GHAR CHOTAA HAI.

CHOTAA GHAR ACHCHHAA HAI.

Note :

Interrogation is expressed by using क्या (Kyaa) at the beginning of a sentence.

क्या यह कलम है?　　　　Kyaa ye(h) kalam hai?　　　Is this a pen?

क्या वहां बच्चे हैं?　　　　Kyaa vahaa(n) bachche hai(n)? Are there children?

वे घर बड़े हैं।

घर में बच्चा है।

चाय गरम है।

क्या काफ़ी भी गरम है?

यह कपड़ा सफ़ेद है।

क्या कपड़ा काला है?

वह बिल्ली है।

क्या बिल्ली सफेद है?

वहां कौन हैं?

वहां कितने बच्चे हैं?

क्या वहां बच्चियां भी हैं?

क्या यह तुम्हारा घर है?

क्या वह भी तुम्हारा घर है?

क्या तुम्हारा घर बड़ा है?

वे घर छोटे नहीं हैं।

घर में चार कमरे हैं।

चाय ठंडी नहीं है।

जी हां, काफ़ी भी गरम है।

काफ़ी ठंडी नहीं है।

क्या कपड़ा साफ़ है?

जी हां, कपड़ा साफ है।

जी नहीं, कपड़ा काला नहीं है।

बिल्ली छोटी है।

बिल्ली काली है।

जी नहीं, बिल्ली काली है।

वहां बच्चे हैं।

वहां बहुत बच्चे हैं।

जी हां, वहां बच्चियां भी हैं।

जी हां, यह मेरा घर है।

जी नहीं, वह मेरा घर नहीं है।

जी नहीं, मेरा घर छोटा है।

छोटा घर अच्छा है

However क्या (Kyaa) is generally dropped while speaking since the tone can express the interrogation.

वहां बच्चे हैं?   Vahaa(n) bachche hai(n)?

To say 'Yes' or 'No' in the beginning of the sentence we should use जी हां (Jee Haa(n)) or जी नहीं (Jee Nahee(n)). जी (Jee) can also be dropped.

जी (Jee) indicates respect.

Lesson 5

I. Shabd (Words) :

Nouns :

Somvaar	Mangalvaar	Budhvaar	Guruvaar	Şukravaar	Şanivar
Monday	Tuesday	Wednesday	Thursday	Friday	Saturday
Ravivar/Itvaar	Sunday				
Din	day/day-time		Saberaa	morning	
Şaam	evening		Raat	night	
Dopahar	afternoon		Sabere	in the morning	
Dopahar ko	in the afternoon		Şaam ko	in the evening	
Raat ko	at night	Din me(n)	in the day-time/in a day		
Haftaa	week	Maheenaa	month		
Saal/Baras	year				

II. Sentences (Present tense) :

My(n) Hindi seekhthaa hoo(n)/seekhtee hoo(n)	I learn Hindi.
Kyaa tum bhee Hindi seekhthe ho/seekhthee ho?	Do you also learn Hindi?
Jee Haa(n); my(n) bhee Hindi seekhthaa hoo(n)/ seekhthee hoo(n)	Yes; I too learn Hindi
Mera bhaayee sabere doodh peethaa hai	My brother drinks milk in the morning.
Meree behan doodh nahee(n) peethee hai; chaai peethee hai.	My sister does not drink milk; (she) drinks tea.
Bachchaa kamre me(n) sothaa hai (M.S.)	The child sleeps in the room.
Bachche kamre me(n) sothe hai(n) (M.Pl.)	The children sleep in the room
Bachachee kamre me(n) sothee hai. (F.S.)	The child sleeps in the room.
Bachchiyaa(n) kamre me(n) sothee hai(n) (F.Pl.)	The children sleep in the room.

पाठ-5

I   **शब्द :**

Nouns

सोमवार	मंगलवार	बुधवार	गुरुवार
शुक्रवार	शनिवार	रविवार/इतवार	
दिन	सबेरा		
शाम	रात		
दोपहर	सबेरे		
दोपहर को	शाम को		
रात को	दिन में		
हफ़्ता	महीना		
साल/बरस			

II   **वाक्य :**

मैं हिन्दी सीखता हूं/सीखती हूं।
क्या तुम भी हिन्दी सीखते हो/सीखती हो?
जी हां, मैं भी हिन्दी सीखता हूं/सीखती हूं।
मेरा भाई सबेरे दूध पीता है।
मेरी बहन दूध नहीं पीती है; चाय पीती है।
बच्चा कमरे में सोता है।
बच्चे कमरे में सोते हैं।
बच्ची कमरे में सोती है।
बच्चियां कमरे में सोती हैं।

Hum log mydaan me(n) khelthe hai(n)	We play in the playground
My(n) roz sabere kasrat karthaa hoo(n)	I do exercise daily in the morning.
Meree behane(n) sabere sangeet seekhthee hai(n)	My sisters learn music in the morning

III. Prepositions :

(Prepositions in Hindi are used after the noun or pronoun, hence post-positions)

1. **Ko = to (in the sense of giving/teaching something to somebody)**

    'Ko' is also used to indicate an animate object.

My(n) behan ko bhent* dethaa hoo(n)	I give a gift to the sister.
Doctor mareez ko dekhthaa hai	Doctor sees a patient
Hum chaaval* khaathe hai(n)	We eat rice

    * rice = inanimate object.

2. **Se = by/with (indicates the instrument); from**

Hum gaaḍee* se aathe hai(n)	We come by a vehicle
My(n) kalam se likhthee hoo(n)	I write with a pen
Ve ghar se yahaa(n) aathe hai(n)	They come here from home

[Note : M.S. = Masculine Singular; M.Pl. = Maculine plural; F.S. = Feminine Singular; F.Pl. = Feminine Plural]

Note:

1. I go to school = My(n) school jaathaa hoo(n)

    She comes to the house = Vo ghar aathee hai.

    Whereas in English 'To' is used in the sense of 'going or coming to', no preposition is used in Hindi on such occasions.

2. Kaa (का) is used when the noun following is masculine singular.

    Ke (के) is used when the noun following is masculine plural.

    Kee (की) is used when the noun following is feminine singular or plural.

Joseph's House	जोसफ़ का घर	Joseph Ka ghar
Joseph's Houses	जोसफ़ के घर	Joseph ke ghar
Joseph's book	जोसफ़ की किताब	Joseph kee kitaab
Joseph's books	जोसफ़ की किताबें	Joseph kee kitaabe(n)

(Continued on next page)

हम लोग मैदान में खेलते हैं।

मैं रोज़ सबेरे कसरत करता हूं।

मेरी बहनें सबेरे संगीत सीखती हैं।

III Prepositions :

1. को = To

    मैं बहन को भेंट देता हूं।

    डाक्टर मरीज़ को देखता है।

    हम चावल खाते हैं

2. से = By, With, From

    हम गाड़ी से आते हैं।

    मैं कलम से लिखती हूं।

    वे घर से यहां आते हैं।

---

3. A. When a masculine singular noun ending with 'aa' is followed by a preposition, 'aa' changes into 'e'.

    Ladkaa Ko = Ladke ko

    Ghodaa par = Ghode par

    Kamraa me(n) = Kamre me(n)

    No other singular noun (masculine or feminine) will change.

    Ghar me(n) = Ghar me(n)

    Ladkee ko = Ladkee ko

    Ped par = Ped par

    Kursee par = Kursee par

    Paanee me(n) = Paanee me(n)

    Aadmee (man) ka = Aadmee ka

    B. All plural nouns whether they are masculine or feminine, will change to 'o(n)' irrespective of their ending.

    Ladke ko = Ladko(n) ko

    Ghode par = Ghodo(n) par

    Ghar (pl.) me(n) = Gharo(n) me(n)

    Aadamee (men) ka = Aadmiyo(n) ka

    Ladkiyaa(n) ko = Ladkiyo(n) ko

    Kursiyaa(n) par = Kursiyo(n) par

(Continued on next page.)

3. Me(n) = in Par = on

Ghar me(n)	in the house
Zameen par	on the floor

4. Kaa (m.s.)/Ke (m.pl.) /Kee (f.s. & pl.) = of (possessive preposition)

Anita kaa bhaayee	Anita ke bhaayee
Anita's brother	Anita's brothers
Ram kee behan	Ram kee behne(n)
Ram's sister	Ram's sisters

C. If the noun ending with 'aa' is preceded by an adjective ending with 'aa' and the noun is followed by a preposition both will change to 'e'

Achchhaa ladkaa ko = Achchhe ladke ko

When the noun is masculine plural or feminine singular or plural, the adjective will have the usual change; of course, feminine adjective ending with 'ee' will remain the same in both singular and plural.

Example :

Achche ladko(n) ko
Chotee kursee par
Chotee kursiyo(n) par

3. में in   पर on
   घर में   ज़मीन पर

4. का/के/की = of (possessive preposition)
   अनीता **का** भाई   अनीता **के** भाई
   राम **की** बहन   राम **की** बहनें

Lesson 6

I. Shabd (Words) :

(A) *Oopar above/up Neeche under/down/below Andar inside Baahar outside
Saamne in front Peechhe behind Pehle before Baad after

(B) (Verbal Nouns) :

aanaa   coming jaanaa   going   khaanaa eating   gaanaa   singing
laanaa   bringing byttnaa sitting   uttnaa   getting up/rising/waking
dekhnaa seeing   sunnaa   hearing/listening   bolnaa   speaking
seekhnaa learning sonaa   sleeping   ronaa   crying

(C) Learn the following :

ke saath	along with/together with	ke liye	for
ke binaa	without	ke alaavaa	in addition
ke sivaa	except	Ke paas	near

पाठ-6

I   **शब्द :**

अ)   ऊपर   नीचे   अन्दर   बाहर
       सामने   पीछे   पहले   बाद

आ)   आना   जाना   खाना   गाना
       लाना   बैठना   उठना
       देखना   सुनना   बोलना
       सीखना   सोना   रोना

इ)   के साथ   के लिये
       के बिना   के अलावा
       के सिवा   के पास

II. Sentences (Review) : (Use of prepositions)

1. Behan bhaayee ko bhe(n)t dethee hai.

   Adhyaapak Mohan ko Hindi sikhaathe hai(n).   **adhyaapak = teacher**

   Tum dost ko kyaa dethe ho?

   My(n) dost ko Hindi kitaab dethaa hoo(n).

2. Mere pitajee daftar se aathe hai(n).   Ve ladkiyaa(n) ghar se aathee hai(n)

   daftar = office

   My(n) kalam se likhthee hoo(n)   Hum aankho(n) se dekhthe hai(n)

   Log rel gaadee se ghar jaathe hai(n)

3. Bachche ghar me(n) kaam karthe hai(n).   Meraa bhaayee mydaan me(n)
                                                    khelthaa hai

   Bachchiyaa(n) kamre me(n) sothee hai(n)   Hum log kursee par bytthe hai(n)

   Deevaar par kyaa hai?   Deevar par tasveere(n) hai(n).

   Deevaar = wall   **Tasveer = picture**

4. Mere bhaayee kaa ghar sahar me(n) hai.

   Hindustan kaa naam bharat bhee hai.

   Vahaan(n) meree behno(n) ke teen ghar hai(n).

   Sheela kaa bhaayee vahaa(n) hai.   Sheela ke do bhaayee ghar me(n) hai(n).

   Sheela kee behan bheee Ghar me(n) hai.   Sheela kee behne(n) dookaan me(n) hai(n).

   Dookaan = shop / store

III. Javaab deejiye : (Please give answer/s)

Aap log yahaa(n) kitne baje aathe hai(n)?

Aapke darje me(n) kitnee ladkiyaa (n) hai(n)?   Darjaa = class

Kyaa ye(h) tumhaaraa kamraa hai?   Kyaa tumhaaraa kamraa badaa hai?

Tumhaare kamre me(n) kitnee khidkiyaa(n) hai(n)?

Kamre me(n) kitne bachche hai(n)?   Ve kyaa karthe hai(n)?

Tum raat ko kyaa kaathee ho? Tum raat ko kitne baje sothee ho?

Hum yahaan(n) kyo(n) aathe hai(n)? Hum restaurant kyo(n) jaathe hai(n)?

Hum pustakaalay kyo(n) jaathe hai(n)? pustakaalay = library, kyo(n) = why

II   Sentences (Review) :

1. बहन भाई को भेंट देती है।
    अध्यापक मोहन को हिन्दी सिखाते हैं।
    तुम दोस्त को क्या देते हो?
    मैं दोस्त को हिन्दी किताब देता हूं।

2. मेरे पिताजी दफ़्तर से आते हैं।   वे लड़कियां घर से आती हैं।
    मैं कलम से लिखती हूं।   हम आंखों से देखते हैं।
    लोग रेल गाड़ी से घर जाते हैं।

3. **बच्चे घर में काम करते हैं?**   **मेरा भाई मैदान में खेलता है।**
    बच्चियां कमरे में सोती हैं।   **हम लोग कुरसी पर बैठते हैं।**
    दीवार पर क्या है?   **दीवार पर तसवीरें हैं।**

4. मेरे भाई का घर शहर में है।
    हिन्दुस्तान का नाम भारत भी है।
    वहां मेरी बहनों के तीन घर हैं।
    शीला का भाई वहां है।   शीला के दो भाई घर में हैं।
    शीला की बहन भी घर में है।   शीला की बहनें दूकान में हैं।

III   जवाब दीजिये :

आप लोग यहां कितने बजे आते हैं?
आपके दर्जे में कितनी लड़कियां हैं?
क्या यह तुम्हारा कमरा है?   क्या तुम्हारा कमरा बड़ा है?
तुम्हारे कमरे में कितनी खिड़कियां हैं?
कमरे में कितने बच्चे हैं   वे क्या करते हैं?
तुम रात को क्या खाती हो?   तुम रात को कितने बजे सोती हो?
हम यहां क्यों आते हैं?   हम रेस्तोरां क्यों जाते हैं?
हम पुस्तकालय क्यों जाते हैं?

*Note : These words can be used independently. When used with a noun or pronoun, they should be preceded by 'Ke'.

Example :

(a)   Oopar aasmaan hai = Sky is above

Andar aao = Come inside

(b)   Peḍ ke oopar bandar hai = A monkey is on (above) the tree

Ghar ke andar aao = Come inside the house.

Bageechaa makaan ke saamne hai = A garden is in front of the building.

COMBINATION OF CONSONANTS :

प् + य = प्य	Pya	म् + य + म्य	Mya
ग् + य = ग्य	Gya	च् + य = च्य	Chya
व् + य = व्य	Vya	त् + य = त्य	Tya
प् + प = प्प	Ppa	च् + छ = च्छ	Chcha
त् + त = त्त	Ththa		
स् + त = स्त	Sta		
ष् + ण = ष्ण	Shna	ष् + ट = ष्ट	Shta

Some exceptions

ट् + ट = ट्ट, ट्ट	Tta	ल् + ल = ल्ल	Lla
ट् + ठ = ट्ठ, ट्ठ	Ttta	क् + य = क्य	Kya
ट् + र = ट्र	Tra	क् + म = क्म	Kma
क् + र = क्र	Kra	र् + क = र्क	Rka
प् + र = प्र	Pra	र् + प = र्प	Rpa
म् + र = म्र	Mra	र् + म = र्म	Rma
स् + र = स्र	Sra	र् + स = र्स	Rsa
व् + र = व्र	Vra	र् + व = र्व	Rva
श् + र = श्र	Ṣra	र् + श = र्श	Rṣa

Lesson 7

1. **Naye Shabd (New Words) :**

Jaldee	quickly	Der se	belatedly/late	Tez	fast/sharp
Dheere-Dheere	slowly	Samay Par	on time	Achaanak	suddenly
Kabhee/Kabhee-Kabhee	sometimes			Hameshaa	always
Kyo(n)	why	Kyonki	because	Isliye	therefore
Lekin	but	Sust	lazy	Chust	active / tight
Sach	truth	Sachchaa	true	Jhoott	lie (untruth)
Jhootta	false/untrue	Sundar/Khoobsoorat	beautiful		
Meettaa	sweet (adjective)	Mittaayee*	sweet (n)		

II. Use of **Thaa   The   Thee   Thee(n)   (was/were)**
          (m.s.)   (m.pl.)   (f.s.)   (f.pl.)
          (These are the past tense forms of 'To Be'.)

Aaj Budhvaar hai.	Today is Wednesday.
Kal Mangalvaar thaa	Yesterday was Tuesday.
Aaj my(n) yahaa(n) hoo(n).	I am here today.
Kal my(n) ghar me(n) thaa (thee).	Yesterday I was in the house (at home)
Tum kal kahaa(n) the / (thee(n)).	Where were you yesterday?
Kal my(n) shahar me(n) thaa / thee.	Yesterday I was in the city.
Bachchaa kamre me(n) thaa.	A child (m) was in the room.
Bachche kamre me(n) the	Children were in the room.
Bachchee kamre me(n) thee	A child (f) was in the room.
Bachchiyaa(n) kamre me(n) thee(n)	Children were in the room.
Meree maa(n) school me(n) thee	My mother was in the school.
Meree behne(n) bhee school me(n) thee(n).	My Sisters were also in the school.

पाठ-7

I **नये शब्द :**

जल्दी	देर से	तेज़
धीरे-धीरे	समय पर	अचानक
कभी/कभी-कभी	हमेशा	क्यों
क्योंकि	इसलिए	लेकिन
सुस्त	चुस्त	सच
सच्चा	झूठ	झूठा
सुन्दर/खूबसूरत	मीठा	मिठाई

II **था, थे, थी, थीं**

आज बुधवार है।

कल मंगलवार था।

आज मैं यहां हूं।

कल मैं घर में था/थी।

तुम कल कहां थे/थीं?

कल मैं शहर में था/थी।

बच्चा कमरे में था।

बच्चे कमरे में थे।

बच्ची कमरे में थी।

बच्चियां कमरे में थीं।

मेरी मां स्कूल में थी।

मेरी बहनें भी स्कूल में थीं।

Meraa bhaayee vahaa(n) nahee(n) thaa.	My brother was not there.
Mere do bhaayee mydaan me(n) the.	My two brothers were in the playground.

**III. Javaab deejiye : (Please give answers)

a. Tum kahaan(n) rahthee ho?

Aap yahaa(n) kyaa seekhthee hai(n)?

Hum log yahaa(n) kitne baje aathe hai(n)?

Hum log yahaa(n) kyo(n) aathe hai(n)?

Aap dost ko kyaa dethee hai(n)?

Aap Kahaa(n) se Aathe hai(n)?

Bachchaa kahaa(n) khelthaa hai?

b. Bachcha kyaa kar rahaa hai?

Bachche kyaa likh rahe hai(n)?

Bachche mydaan me(n) kyaa kar rahe hai(n)?

Tumharee behan kahaa(n) jaa rahee hai?

Tumharee behne(n) kyaa likh rahee hai(n)?

Aapkee billee kyaa pee rahee hai?

Kyaa ve bachchiyaa(n) tasveer banaa rahee hai(n)?

IV. Vaakya (Sentences) : Review

Bhaarat baḍaa desh hai.

Bhaarat ke paas Pakistan hai. (ke paas = near)

Bhaarat ke paas Sri Lanka bhee hai.

Humaaree bahan maa ke saath mandir jaathee hai. (Mandir = Temple)

(ke saath = along with/together with)

Meraa dost mere saath hamesha Hindi me(n) bolthaa hai.

Ghar ke saamne (aage) yeh sundar bageechaa hai. Sundar = beaut

(Ke saamne/Ke aage = in front of)

Ghar ke peechhe bhee sundar bageechaa hai.   (Ke peeche = behind)

Makaan ke neeche rel gaadee jaathee hai.   (Ke neeche = below/under)

Sadak ke oopar bhee rel gaadee jaathee hai.   (Ke oopar = above)

मेरा भाई वहां नहीं था।

मेरे दो भाई मैदान में थे।

III **जवाब दीजिये** :

a.   तुम कहां रहती हो?

आप यहां क्या सीखती हैं?

हम लोग यहां कितने बजे आते हैं?

हम लोग यहां क्यों आते हैं?

आप दोस्त को क्या देती हैं?

आप कहां से आते हैं?

बच्चा कहां खेलता है?

b.   बच्चा क्या कर रहा है?

बच्चे क्या लिख रहे हैं?

बच्चे मैदान में क्या कर रहे हैं?

तुम्हारी बहन कहां जा रही है?

तुम्हारी बहनें क्या लिख रही हैं?

आपकी बिल्ली क्या पी रही है?

क्या वे बच्चियां तसवीर बना रही हैं?

IV   **वाक्य** (Review) :

भारत बड़ा देश है।	
भारत **के पास** पाकिस्तान है।	Near
भारत के पास श्रीलंका भी है।	
हमारी बहन मां **के साथ** मंदिर जाती है।	**Along with/Together with**
मेरा दोस्त मेरे साथ हमेशा हिन्दी में बोलता है।	
घर **के सामने** (आगे) एक सुन्दर बगीचा है।	In front of
घर **के पीछे** भी सुन्दर बगीचा है।	Behind
मकान **के नीचे** रेल गाड़ी जाती है।	Below/Under
सड़क **के ऊपर** भी रेल गाड़ी जाती है।	Above

My(n) kakshaa **ke baad** ghar jaathee hoo(n)?   Ke baad = after

My(n) yek saal **ke pehle** yahaa(n) nahee(n) thaa.   ke pehle = before

Bachchaa ghar **ke andar** khelthaa hai.   Ke andar = inside

Yek gaadee dafthar **ke baahar** hai.   Ke baahar = outside

V. Khalee jagahe(n) bhariye : **(Fill in the blanks)**

Hum kalam _____ likhthe hai(n).

Vo kursee _____ byttthaa hai.

Meree behan _____ naam Reeta hai.

Aap dost _____ kithaab deejiye.

Bachche mydaan _____ khelthe hai(n).

Tum kahaa(n) _____ Aathe ho?

Vo _____ panee peethaa hai.

Aaj Budhvaar _____

Kal Mangalvaar _____

Tum school me(n) kayaa _____ ?

Vo ghar_____tasveer banathaa hai.

Aap andar _____

Tum vahan(n) _____

** Note :

A. Verbs in present tense, are followed by suffixes ता (Thaa) ते (Te) and ती (Tee) –

Masculine :

My(n) paanee peethaa hoo(n).   I drink water.

Hum paanee peethe hai(n).   We drink water.

Feminine:

Bachchee khelthee hai.   A child plays

Bachchiyaa(n) khelthee hai(n).   Children play

B. To use the verbs in present continuous tense, suffixes रहा (Rahaa), रहे (Rahe) and रही (Rahee) should be added to the verb roots in masculine singular, plural and feminine singular & plural respectively.

(Continued on next page.)

मैं कक्षा **के बाद** घर जाती हूं।	After
मैं एक साल **के पहले** यहां नहीं था।	Before
बच्चा घर **के अन्दर** खेलता है।	Inside
एक गाड़ी दफ़्तर **के बाहर** है।	Outside

V खाली जगहें भरिये :

हम कलम _____ लिखते हैं।

वह कुरसी _____ बैठता है।

मेरी बहन _____ नाम रीता है।

आप दोस्त _____ किताब दीजिये।

बच्चे मैदान _____ खेलते हैं।

तुम कहां _____ आते हो?

वह _____ पानी पीता है।

आज बुधवार _____ ।

कल मंगलवार _____ ।

तुम स्कूल में क्या_____ _____?

वह घर _____ तसवीर बनाता है।

आप अन्दर _____ ।

तुम वहां _____ ।

Masculine singular and plural:

Bachchaa so rahaa hai.	A child is sleeping.
Bachche so rahe hai(n).	Children are sleeping.

Feminine singular and plural:

Bachchee so rahee hai.	A child is sleeping.
Bachchiyaa(n) so rahee hai(n).	Children are sleeping.

Masculine singular and plural:

My(n) padh rahaa hoo(n).	I am reading.
Hum padh rahe hai(n).	We are reading.

Feminine singular and plural:

My(n) padh rahee hoo(n).	I am reading.
Hum padh rahee hai(n).	We are reading.

Lesson 8

(Review lesson)

I. Adverbs:

Ghoḍaa tez dauḍthaa hai.	tez = Fast
Kachuaa dheere dheere chalthaa hai.	kachuaa = tortoise, dheere dheere = slowly.
Tum kakshaa me(n) samay par aao.	samay par = on time
Tum kabhee der se mat aao.	der se = late
Vo Laḍkee khoob gaathee hai.	khoob = very well
Panee zor se barasthaa hai.	zor se = heavily
Bachche aaraam se sothe hai(n).	aaraam se = comfortably
Hum yahaa(n) baraabar aathe hai(n).	baraabar = regularly
Ve aksar ṣahar jaathe hai(n).	aksar = frequently

II. Answer:

Hum dekhthe hai(n)	Kyse? (Kyse = How)
Hum saans lethe hai(n)	Kyse?
Hum bolthe hai(n)	Kyse?
Aaj kyaa din hai?	Kal kyaa din thaa?
Bachcha kya kartha hai?	Mydan me(n) kaun khelte hai(n)?
Aapki behan kitne baje school jaathee hai?	Aap kab ghar jaathee hai(n)?
Aap yahaa(n) kyaa karthee hai(n)?	
Tumharee maa(n) kyaa kar rahee hai?	
Tum sabere kyaa khaathe ho?	Bachchaa kyaa peetha hai?
Tum dost ko kyaa dethee ho?	Tum yahaa(n) kyaa seekhthee ho?
Yahaa(n) kitne log aathe hai(n)?	

Note : Saans le = to breathe

पाठ 8

(Review lesson)

I. **Adverbs :**

घोड़ा तेज़ दौड़ता है।
कछुआ धीरे-धीरे चलता है।
तुम कक्षा में समय पर आओ।
तुम कभी देर से मत आओ।
वह लड़की खूब गाती है।
पानी ज़ोर से बरसता है।
बच्चे आराम से सोते हैं।
हम यहां बराबर आते हैं।
वे अकसर शहर जाते हैं।

II. **जवाब दो :**

हम देखते हैं।	कैसे?
हम सांस लेते हैं।	कैसे?
हम बोलते हैं।	कैसे?
आज क्या दिन है?	कल क्या दिन था?
बच्चा क्या करता है?	मैदान में कौन खेलते हैं?
आपकी बहन कितने बजे स्कूल जाती है?	आप कब घर जाती हैं?
आप यहां क्या करती हैं?	
तुम्हारी मां क्या कर रही है?	
तुम सबेरे क्या खाते हो?	बच्चा क्या पीता है?
तुम दोस्त को क्या देती हो?	तुम यहां क्या सीखती हो?
यहां कितने लोग आते हैं?	

III. Fill in the blanks :

Mahatma Gandhi Bhaarat ke netaa _____   (was)

Martin Luther King Junior America ke netaa _____   (was)

Maa(n) rasoyee ghar me(n) ___   (is)

Vo ghar me(n) kaam ___ hai   (does)

Vo kamra _____ nahee(n) hai   (small)

Aaj Bhaarat ____ hai   (free/independent)

America _____ desh hai   (big)

Meree maa(n) bahut ____ hai   (good)

Bachche _____ andar khelthe hai(n)   (daily)

Note :   Netaa = Leader

Rasoyee ghar = Kitchen

Aazad = free / Independent

III. **खाली जगहें भरिये :**

महात्मा गांधी भारत के नेता _____ ।

मार्टिन लूथर किंग जूनियर अमेरिका के नेता _____ । .

मां रसोई घर में _____ ।

वह घर में काम _____ है।

वह कमरा _____ नहीं है।

आज भारत _____ है।

अमेरिका _____ देश है।

मेरी मां बहुत _____ है।

बच्चे _____ अन्दर खेलते हैं।

Lesson 9

I.   Naye Shabd (New Words) :

Adjectives :

Lambaa = long / tall	Chaudaa = wide	
Oonchaa = high	Nataa = short (in stature)	Motaa = fat
Pathlaa = thin	Halkaa = light (in weight)	**Bhaaree = heavy (in weight)**
Beemar = sick	Tandurust = Healthy	Kamzor = weak
Mazboot = strong	Meettaa = sweet	Theekhaa = spicy/hot
Namkeen = salty	Kaduvaa/Kadvaa = bitter	
Aasaan = easy	Muskil = difficult	Gehraa = deep

II.   Padhiye aur samajhiye (Read and understand) :

Hum hafthe me(n) yek din yahaa(n) aathe hai(n).

Hum log yahaa(n) Hindi seekhthe hai(n).

Ve log Hindi bol rahe hai(n).

Ve log Hindi seekhne ke liye yahaa(n) aathe hai(n).

Aap kal kahaa(n) jaa rahee thee(n)?   (past continuous form)*

My(n) kal sahar jaa rahee thee.   (past continuous form)

Meree saheliyaa(n) sahar me(n) rahthee hai(n).

Humaare bhaayee New York me(n) rahthe hai(n).

My(n) hamesaa tandaa paanee peethaa hoo(n).

Aap sabere kyaa peethe hai(n)?

---

*   See the present continuous form under lesson 7. The same pattern is followed in the past continuous form also. Of course, to make it into the continuous past form, we should use Thaa (m.s.), The (m.pl.), Thee (f.s.) and Thee(n) (f.pl.) in the place of Hoo(n), Ho, Hai, and Hai(n) to give the meaning of 'was/were'.

पाठ-9

I नये शब्द :

लंबा	चौड़ा	ऊंचा
नाटा	मोटा	पतला
हलका	भारी	बीमार
तन्दुरुस्त	कमज़ोर	मज़बूत
मीठा	तीखा	नमकीन
कडुवा/कड़वा	आसान	मुश्किल
गहरा		

II पढ़िये और समझिये :

हम हफ़्ते में एक दिन यहां आते हैं।

हम लोग यहां हिन्दी सीखते हैं।

वे लोग हिन्दी बोल रहे हैं।

वे लोग हिन्दी सीखने के लिए यहां आते हैं।

आप कल कहां जा रही थीं?

मैं कल शहर जा रही थी।

मेरी सहेलियां शहर में रहती हैं।

हमारे भाई न्यूयार्क में रहते हैं।

मैं हमेशा ठंडा पानी पीता हूं।

आप सबेरे क्या पीते हैं?

My(n) sabere coffee peethaa hoo(n).

My(n) kabhee kabhee chaai bhee peethaa hoo(n).

Aap kahaa(n) se aa rahe hai(n)?

My(n) dafthar se aa rahaa hoo(n)?

Bachche school se ghar jaa rahe hai(n).

Meree maa(n) mandir jaa rahee hai.

Meree maa(n) ke saath meraa bhayee bhee jaa rahaa hai.

My(n) **apnaa** kaam karthee hoo(n).

Bachche **apnaa** sabak likhthe hai(n).

Aap **apnaa** kaam keejiye.

III. Future Tense (Masculine & Feminine):

Learn

A. My(n) Hindi seekhoongaa/seekhoongee   I will learn Hindi.
    Tum kyaa seekhoge/seekhogee?   What will you learn?
    Vo Hindi seekhegaa/seekhegee   He/She will learn Hindi.
    Hum/Aap/Ve Hindi seekhenge/seekhengee.   We/You/They will learn Hindi.

B. My(n) phal laaoongaa/laaoongee   I will bring fruit.
    Tum kyaa laaoge/laaogee?   What will you bring?
    Vo bhee phal laayegaa/laayegee   He/She will also bring fruit.
    Hum/Aap/Ve bhee phal laayenge/laayengee.   We/You/They will bring fruit.

Note :

A. Future tense of a verb is formed by adding the following suffixes:

My(n) aa **oongaa**   Hum aa **yenge**
Tum kab aa **oge**   Aap kab aa **yenge**
Vo ⎫   Ve ⎫
Ye(h) ⎬ aa **yegaa**   Ye ⎬ aa **yenge**
Kaun ⎭   Kaun ⎭

These are masculine forms. To make them into feminine, change oongaa, oge, yegaa and yenge into oongee, ogee, yegee and yengee respectively.

मैं सबेरे कॉफ़ी पीता हूं।

मैं कभी-कभी चाय भी पीता हूं।

आप कहां से आ रहे हैं?

मैं दफ़्तर से आ रहा हूं।

बच्चे स्कूल से घर जा रहे हैं।

मेरी मां मन्दिर जा रही है।

मेरी मां के साथ मेरा भाई भी जा रहा है।

मैं अपना काम करती हूं।

बच्चे अपना सबक लिखते हैं।

आप अपना, काम कीजिये।

III Future Tense (Masculine & Feminine):

अ) मैं हिन्दी सीखूंगा/सीखूंगी।

तुम क्या सीखोगे/सीखोगी?

वह हिन्दी सीखेगा/सीखेगी।

हम/आप/वे हिन्दी सीखेंगे/सीखेंगी।

आ) मैं फल लाऊंगा/लाऊंगी।

तुम क्या लाओगे/लाओगी।

वह भी फल लायेगा/लायेगी।

हम/आप/वे फल लायेंगे/लायेंगी।

B. Use of Apnaa (अपना) : Apnaa means 'one's own'. When the subject is मैं, तुम, वह, यह, हम, आप, वे or ये, we cannot use the possessive form of the same pronoun in the sentence, instead, we have to use 'Apnaa' uniformly. 'Apnaa' will have to be changed to 'Apne' or 'Apnee' depending upon the gender and number of the noun it qualifies.

My(n) Apnaa sabak paḍhthaa hoo(n)	I read my lesson.
Vo apnee kitaab paḍhthee hai	She reads her book.
Hum apne ghar me(n) rahthe hai(n)	We live in our house.

Lesson 10

(Review Lesson)

1. **Khaalee jagahe(n) bhariye : (Fill in the blanks)**

   Vo .... kamraa hai.

   Kamre .... bachche khel .... hai(n).

   My(n) .... chaai .... hoo(n).

   Aap kal ṣaam ko kyaa ....?

   Aapke .... me(n) kitne kamre hai(n)?

   Hum daftar .... yahaa(n) aathe hai(n).

   Maa(n) bachche .... doodh dethee ....

   Bachchaa doodh ....

   Laḍkiyaa(n) mydaan .... khel .... hai(n).

   My(n) kal chhe baje yahaa(n)....................

   Kyaa tumhaaraa dost kal dookan ....?

   Kal mangalvaar ....

   Budhvaar .... hum Hindi seekhthee ....

II. **Javaab deejiye (Give answers) :**

   Aap kal kahaa(n) the?

   Ab aap kahaa(n) jaa rahe hai(n)?

   Bachche kal shaam ko kahaa(n) the?

   Ve vahaa(n) kyaa kar rahe the?

   Aapke maa(n)-baap parso(n) kahaa(n) jaa rahe the?

   Ve ṣahar me(n) kitne din rahenge?

   Ve vahaa(n) kyaa karenge?

   Tum kal kahaa(n) jaaogee?

   Tumhaare saath kaun-kaun jaayenge?

पाठ 10

(Review Lesson)

I **खाली जगहें भरिये :**

वह .... कमरा है।

कमरे .... बच्चे खेल .... हैं।

मैं............. चाय .... हूं।

आप कल शाम को क्या ....?

आपके .... में कितने कमरे हैं?

हम दफ़्तर .... यहां आते हैं।

मां बच्चे .... दूध देती .... ।

बच्चा दूध .... ।

लड़कियां मैदान .... खेल .... हैं।

मैं कल छे बजे यहां .... ।

क्या तुम्हारा दोस्त कल दूकान ....?

कल मंगलवार .... ।

बुधवार .... हम हिन्दी सीखती .... ।

II **जवाब दीजिये :**

आप कल कहां थे?

अब आप कहां जा रहे हैं?

बच्चे कल शाम को कहां थे?

वे वहां क्या कर रहे थे?

आपके माँ-बाप परसों कहां जा रहे थे?

वे शहर में कितने दिन रहेंगे?

वे वहां क्या करेंगे?

तुम कल कहां जाओगी?

तुम्हारे साथ कौन-कौन जायेंगे?

Bachche kab school jaayenge?

Tum kyaa piogee?

Kyaa tum das baje ghar pahu(n)chogee? Pahu(n)ch = reach

Tumhaare ghar me(n) kitne log rahthe hai(n)?

Kyaa tum roz akhbaar paḍhoge? Akhbaar = newspaper

Tum dookaan me(n) kyaa khareedoge?

Kyaa aajkal baazar me(n) taazee sabziyaa(n) milthee hai(n)? Taazee = fresh

Vo apne dost ke saath kahaa(n) jaa rahaa hai?

Ve log yahaa(n) kab aayenge?

III. Shabd (Words) :

Eeṣwar/Bhagwaan = God

Jaanvar = animal

Ghoḍaa = horse

Bhyns* = buffalo

Hiran = deer

Billee* = cat

Badan/Ṣareer = body

Maathaa = forehead

Gaal = cheek

Naak* = nose

Baa(n)h* = arm

Ghutnaa = knee

Pyr = leg

Aadmee = man

Pakshee/Chiḍiyaa* = bird

Gaai* = cow

Bakree* = goat

Ṣer = lion

Choohaa = mouse

Sir = head

Kandhaa = shoulder

Galaa = throat

Aankh* = eye

Haath = hand

U(n)glee* = finger

Aurat* = woman

Haathee = elephant

Byl = bull

Bandar = monkey

Baagh = tiger

Kuththaa = dog

Baal = hair

Gardan* = neck

Chibuk = chin

Kaan = ear

Pet = stomach

A(n)gootta = thumb

Dhanyavaad/Ṣhukriyaa = Thanks

बच्चे कब स्कूल जायेंगे?

तुम क्या पिओगी?

क्या तुम दस बजे घर पहुंचोगी?

तुम्हारे घर में कितने लोग रहते हैं?

क्या तुम रोज़ अखबार पढ़ोगे?

तुम दूकान में क्या खरीदोगे?

क्या आजकल बाज़ार में ताज़ी सब्जियां मिलती हैं?

वह अपने दोस्त के साथ कहां जा रहा है?

वे लोग यहां कब आयेंगे?

III **शब्द :**

ईश्वर/भगवान	आदमी	औरत*
जानवर	पक्षी/चिड़िया*	हाथी
घोड़ा	गाय*	बैल
भैंस*	बकरी*	बंदर
हिरन	शेर	बाघ
बिल्ली*	चूहा	कुत्ता
बदन/शरीर	सिर	बाल
माथा	कंधा	गरदन*
गाल	गला	चिबुक
नाक*	आंख*	कान
बांह*	हाथ	पेट
घुटना	उंगली*	अंगूठा
पैर		

धन्यवाद/शुक्रिया

Verbs in defferent forms/tenses(masculine and feminine & singular and plural)

Chart

Jaa = go

Present	Present continuous	Past continuous	Future
My(n) jaathaa hoo(n)	jaa raha hoo(n)	jaa rahaa thaa	jaaoo(n)gaa
jaathee hoo(n)	jaa rahee hoo(n)	jaa rahee thee	jaaoo(n)gee
Tum jaathe ho	jaa rahe ho	jaa rahe the	jaaoge
jaathee ho	jaa rahee ho	jaa rahee thee(n)	jaaogee
Vo/Ye(h)/Kaun (m) jaathaa hai	jaa rahaa hai	jaa rahaa thaa	jaayegaa
Vah/Ye(h)/Kaun (f) jaathee hai	jaa rahee hai	jaa rahee thee	jaayegee
Hum } jaathe hai(n)	jaa rahe hai(n)	jaa rahe the	jaaye(n)ge
Aap/Ve/Ye } jaathee hai(n)	jaa rahee hai(n)	jaa rahee thee(n)	jaaye(n)gee
Kaun (pl.) }			

Kar = do

My(n) karthaa hoo(n)	kar rahaa hoo(n)	kar rahaa thaa	karoo(n)gaa
karthee hoo(n)	kar rahee hoo(n)	kar rahee thee	karoo(n)gee
Tum karthe ho	kar rahe ho	kar rahe the	karoge
Karthee ho	kar rahee ho	kar rahee thee(n)	karogee
Vo/Ye(h)/Kaun (m) Karthaa hai	kar rahaa hai	kar rahaa thaa	karegaa
Vo/Ye(h)/Kaun (f) karthee hai	kar rahee hai	kar rahee thee	karegee
Hum } karthe hai(n)	kar rahe hai(n)	kar rahe the	kare(n)ge
Aap/Ve/Ye/ } karthee hai(n)	kar rahee hai(n)	kar rahee thee(n)	kare(n)gee
Kaun (pl.) }			

Verbs in different forms/tenses (masculine and feminine & singular and plural)

Chart

जा

Present	Present continuous	Past continuous	Future
मैं जाता हूं	जा रहा हूं	जा रहा था	जाऊंगा
जाती हूं	जा रही हूं	जा रही थी	जाऊंगी
तुम जाते हो	जा रहे हो	जा रहे थे	जाओगे
जाती हो	जा रही हो	जा रही थीं	जाओगी
वह/यह/कौन (m) जाता है	जा रहा है	जा रहा था	जायेगा
वह/यह/कौन (f) जाती है	जा रही है	जा रही थी	जायेगी
हम } जाते हैं	जा रहे हैं	जा रहे थे	जायेंगे
आप/वे/ये/कौन (pl) } जाती हैं	जा रही हैं	जा रही थीं	जायेंगी

कर

Present	Present continuous	Past continuous	Future
मैं करता हूं	कर रहा हूं	कर रहा था	करूंगा
करती हूं	कर रही हूं	कर रही थी	करूंगी
तुम करते हो	कर रहे हो	कर रहे थे	करोगे
करती हो	कर रही हो	कर रही थीं	करोगी
वह/यह/कौन (m) } करता है	कर रहा है	कर रहा था	करेगा
वह/यह/कौन (f) } करती है	कर रही है	कर रही थी	करेगी
हम/आप } करते हैं	कर रहे हैं	कर रहे थे	करेंगे
वे/ये/कौन (pl) } करती हैं	कर रही हैं	कर रही थीं	करेंगी

Part II

Hindi Course (Intermediate)

Session II

10 Lessons

Session II (Intermediate)

Lesson 1

I.   Read :

Ye(h) havaayee addaa hai.	This is airport.
Meree behan California se aanewalee hai.	My sister is coming (about to come) from California.
My(n) use lene ke liye havaayee addaa pahu(n)chaa.	I reached the airport to receive her.
Vahaa(n) bahut log the.	There were many people.
Ve sab apnee apnee zabaan me(n) bol rahe the.	They were all speaking in their own languages.
Koyee English me(n), koyee Spanish me(n), koyee German me(n), koyee French me(n), koyee Chinese me(n), koyee Hindi me(n) aur koyee Punjabi me(n) bol rahe the.	Some were speaking in English, some in Spanish, some in German, some in French, some in Chinese, some in Hindi and some were speaking in Punjabi.
Sabke rishtedaar alag alag jagaho(n) se aa rahe the.	**The relatives of all were coming from different places.**
My(n) ghar se chaar baje niklaa aur saaḍhe paa(n)ch baje havaayee addaa pahu(n)chaa.	I started from home at 4 o'clock and reached the airport at 5:30.
Meree maa(n) bhee mere saath thee.	My mother was also with me.
Havaayee jahaaz aadhaa ghantaa der se pahu(n)chaa.	The flight reached half an hour late.

दूसरा सत्र (मध्यम स्तर)

पाठ-1

I   **पढ़िये :**

यह हवाई अड्डा है।

मेरी बहन कैलीफ़ोर्निया से आनेवाली है।

मैं उसे लेने के लिए हवाई अड्डा पहुंचा।

वहां बहुत लोग थे।

वे सब अपनी-अपनी ज़बान में बोल रहे थे।

कोई इंग्लिश में, कोई स्पेनिश में, कोई जर्मन में,
कोई फ़्रेंच में, कोई चीनी में, कोई हिन्दी में और कोई
पंजाबी में बोल रहे थे।

सबके रिश्तेदार अलग-अलग जगहों से आ रहे थे।

मैं घर से चार बजे निकला और साढ़े पांच बजे हवाई अड्डा पहुंचा।

मेरी मां भी मेरे साथ थी।

हवाई जहाज़ आधा घंटा देर से पहुंचा।

Thoḍee der me(n) meree behan bhee aa gayee.	In a shortwhile, my sister also came.
Hum sab usse milkar bahut khush huye.	We all were happy to meet her.
Phir my(n), behan aur maa(n) ghar ke liye Taxi se nikle.	Then I, sister and mother left for home by taxi.

II. Past Tense Forms :

	Verb root	M.S.	M.Pl.	F.S.	F.Pl.	
(a)	AA	aayaa	aaye	aayee	aayee(n)	came
	SO	soyaa	soye	soyee	soyee(n)	slept
	BYTT	byttaa	bytte	byttee	byttee(n)	sat
	DAUḌ	daudaa	dauḍe	daudee	daudee(n)	ran
(b)	DEKH	dekhaa	dekhe	dekhee	dekhee(n)	saw
	SUN	sunaa	sune	sunee	sunee(n)	heard
	KHAA	khaayaa	khaaye	khaayee	khaayee(n)	ate
	LAA	Laayaa	Laaye	Laayee	Laayee(n)	brought

Note : See explanations at the bottom of lesson 2

A FEW SENTENCES WITH VERBS IN PAST TENSE :

My(n) yahaa(n) ghar se aayaa/aayee

Hum nau baje ghar pahu(n)che/pahu(n)chee(n)

Bachcha das baje soyaa.	Bachchee das baje soyee.
Bachche das baje soye.	Bachchiyaa(n) das baje soyee(n).
Meraa bhaayee nau baje school gayaa.	Meree behan nau baje school gayee.
Mere teen bhaayee ṣahar gaye.	Meree behne(n) bhee ṣahar gayee(n).

थोड़ी देर में मेरी बहन भी आ गयी।

हम सब उससे मिलकर बहुत खुश हुए।

फिर मैं, बहन और मां घर के लिए टैक्सी से निकले।

II Past Tense forms

a) Verb root	M.S.	M.Pl.	F.S.	F.Pl.	
आ	आया	आये	आयी	आयीं	came
सो	सोया	सोये	सोयी	सोयीं	slept
बैठ	बैठा	बैठे	बैठी	बैठीं	sat
दौड़	दौड़ा	दौड़े	दौड़ी	दौड़ीं	ran
b) देख	देखा	देखे	देखी	देखीं	saw
सुन	सुना	सुने	सुनी	सुनीं	heard
खा	खाया	खाये	खायी	खायीं	ate
ला	लाया	लाये	लायी	लायीं	brought

A few sentences with verbs in past tense

मैं यहां घर से आया/आयी
हम नौ बजे घर पहुंचे/पहुंचीं
बच्चा दस बजे सोया।   बच्ची दस बजे सोयी।
बच्चे दस बजे सोये।   बच्चियां दस बजे सोयीं।
मेरा भाई नौ बजे स्कूल गया।   मेरी बहन नौ बजे स्कूल गयी।
मेरे तीन भाई शहर गये।   मेरी बहनें भी शहर गयीं।

Aap kab yahaa(n) aaye?

My(n) yahaa(n) chhe baje aayaa.

Aapne yahaa(n) kyaa dekhaa?

My(n) ne yahaa(n) kitabae(n) dekhee(n).

My(n) ne kayee akhbaar bhee dekhe.

Tumne shaam ko kyaa kiyaa?

My(n) shaam ko Hindi kakshaa me(n) gayaa.

Vahaa(n) my(n) ne Hindi kahaanee paḍhee.

Meraa bhaayee kal yahaa(n) aayaa.

Mere bhayee ne dookaan me(n)

kayee kapḍe khareede.

My(n) ne bhee kuch cheeze(n) khareedee(n).

Kyaa aapne kuch khareedaa?

Nahee(n), my(n) ne kuch bhee nahee(n) khareedaa.

III. Numbers 1 to 30 (Review) :

1-10	Ek	Do	Teen	Chaar	Paanch
	Chhe	Saat	Aatt	Nau	Dus
11-20	Gyaarah	Baarah	Terah	Chaudah	Pandrah
	Solah	Satrah	Attaarah	Unnees	Bees
21-30	Ikkees	Baayees	Teyees	Chaubees	Pachchees
	Chhabbees	Sattaayees	Attaayees	Untees	Tees

IV. Naye shabd (New words) :

Kabhee/Kabhee-Kabhee	sometimes
Kahee(n)/Kahee(n)-Kahee(n)	somewhere
Kuch-na-kuch	something or the other
Koyee/Koyee na koyee	somebody/someone

kamzor	weak	Mazboot	strong
Beemaar	sick	Tandurust	healthy
Sust	lazy	chust	active/tight
Bachchaa	child	Bachpan	childhood
Javaan	young	Javaanee*	young age
Booḍhaa	old person (m)	Buḍhaapaa	old age
Booḍhee/Buḍhiyaa*	old woman	Duniyaa*/Sansaar	world
Zindagee*/Jeevan	life		

आप कब यहां आये?	मैं यहां छे बजे आया।
आपने यहां क्या देखा?	मैंने यहां किताबें देखीं।
	मैंने कई अखबार भी देखे।
तुमने शाम को क्या किया?	मैं शाम को हिन्दी कक्षा में गया।
	वहां मैंने हिन्दी कहानी पढ़ी।
मेरा भाई कल यहां आया।	मेरे भाई ने दूकान में कई कपड़े खरीदे।
	मैंने भी कुछ चीजें खरीदीं।
क्या आपने कुछ खरीदा?	नहीं, मैंने कुछ भी नहीं खरीदा।

III Numbers 1 - 30 (review)

1-10	एक	दो	तीन	चार	पांच
	छे	सात	आठ	नौ	दस
11-20	ग्यारह	बारह	तेरह	चौदह	पन्द्रह
	सोलह	सत्रह	अठारह	उन्नीस	बीस
21-30	इक्कीस	बाईस	तेईस	चौबीस	पच्चीस
	छब्बीस	सत्ताईस	अड़ाईस	उनतीस	तीस

IV नये शब्द

कभी/कभी-कभी	कहीं/कहीं-कहीं
कुछ-न-कुछ	कोई/कोई-न-कोई
कमज़ोर	मज़बूत
बीमार	तन्दुरुस्त
सुस्त	चुस्त
बच्चा	बचपन
जवान	जवानी*
बूढ़ा	बूढ़ी/बुढ़िया*
बुढ़ापा	दुनिया*/संसार
ज़िन्दगी*/जीवन	

Lesson 2

I. Read :

Ye(h) humaaraa ghar hai. Humaaraa ghar ṣahar me(n) hai.

Humaare ghar me(n) paanch log rahthe hai(n); maa(n), pitaaji, hum do bhaayee and behan.

Humaaraa ghar na chhotaa hai, na baḍaa. Isme(n) aatt kamre hai(n).

Humaare pitaaji vyaapaar karthe hai(n).

Hum dono(n) bhaayee chuttiyo(n) ke din pitaaji kee madad karthe hai(n).

Hum log college me(n) paḍhthe hai(n).

Humaaree maa(n) bahut paḍhee-likhee hai.

Vo paḍhaayee me(n), khaaskar ganit me(n), humaaree sahaaytaa karthee hai.

Pitaa ji roz subah aat baje kaam ke liye nikalthe hai(n) aur shaam ko nau baje ghar
    lautthe hai(n).

Humaaree maa(n) ghar ki dekhbhaal karthee hai.

Humaare ghar ke peeche ek chotaa bageechaa hi. Bageeche me(n) tarah tarah ke phoolo(n)
    ke paudhe hai(n). Hum log hafthe me(n) do din bageeche me(n) kaam karthe
    hai(n). Paudho(n) ko paanee dethe hai(n) aur chaaro(n) taraf safaayee karthe hai(n).
    Humaare bageeche ke phool khushboodaar hai(n).

Kal humaare mama gaa(n)v se aanevaale hai(n)

Hum log unko lene ke liye subah station jaaye(n)ge. Hum apne parivar kee gaaḍee
    me(n) jaaye(n)ge. My(n) gaaḍee chalaaoo(n)gaa. Humaare saath maa(n) aur pitaaji
    bhee ho(n)ge. Meraa chhotaa bhaayee gaaḍee nahee(n) chalaa saktaa. Usne gaaḍee
    chalaanaa nahee(n) seekhaa hai.

Aaj shaam ko zaroore cheeze(n) khareedne ke liye my(n) maa(n) ke saath baazaar
    jaaoo(n)gaa.

Humaaraa parivaar sukhee aur shaant hai.

पाठ-2

I   **पढ़िये :**

यह हमारा घर है। हमारा घर शहर में है।

हमारे घर में पांच लोग रहते हैं; मां, पिताजी, हम दो भाई और बहन।

हमारा घर न छोटा है, न बड़ा। इसमें आठ कमरे हैं।

हमारे पिताजी व्यापार करते हैं।

हम दोनों भाई छुट्टियों के दिन पिताजी की मदद करते हैं।

हम लोग कॉलेज में पढ़ते हैं।

हमारी मां बहुत पढ़ी-लिखी है।

वह पढ़ाई में, खासकर गणित में, हमारी सहायता करती है।

पिताजी रोज़ सुबह आठ बजे काम के लिए निकलते हैं और शाम को नौ बजे घर लौटते हैं।

हमारी मां घर की देखभाल करती है।

हमारे घर के पीछे एक छोटा बगीचा है। बगीचे में तरह-तरह के फूलों के पौधे हैं। हम लोग हफ़्ते में दो दिन बगीचे में काम करते हैं। पौधों को पानी देते हैं और चारों तरफ़ सफ़ाई करते हैं। हमारे बगीचे के फूल खुशबूदार हैं।

कम हमारे मामा गांव से आनेवाले हैं। हम लोग उनको लेने के लिए सुबह स्टेशन जायेंगे। हम अपने परिवार की गाड़ी में जायेंगे। मैं गाड़ी चलाऊंगा। हमारे साथ मां और पिताजी भी होंगे। मेरा छोटा भाई गाड़ी नहीं चला सकता। उसने गाड़ी चलाना नहीं सीखा है।

आज शाम को ज़रूरी चीज़ें खरीदने के लिए मैं मां के साथ बाज़ार जाऊंगा।

हमारा परिवार सुखी और शांत है।

II. Learn these words :

Koshish*	effort	Koshish kar	to try/make an effort
Aashaa*	hope	Aashaa kar	to hope
Madad* / Sahaaytaa*	help	Madad kar/Sahaaytaa kar	to help
Maafee*	pardon/forgiveness	Maaf kar	to pardon/excuse
Der*	delay	Der kar	to delay
Khushee*	happiness	Khush ho	be happy/be pleased
Khush (Adjective)	happy	Khush kar	make happy
Samajh*	understanding	Samajh	to understand
Jeevan	life	Jee	to live
Saa(n)s*	breath	Saa(n)s le	to breathe
Shaayac	perhaps	Achaanak	suddenly
Jaldee jaldee	quickly	Der se	belatedly / late
Anjaane me(n)	unknowingly	Zaroor	surely/definitely
Zarooree	necessary	Zaroorat*	necessity

III. Different Past Tense Forms :

A		B	C		D
Aayaa		Aayaa hai	Aayaa thaa		Aayaa hogaa
came		has come	had come		migh have come
Gayaa		Gayaa hai	Gayaa thaa		Gayaa hogaa
went		has gone	had gone		might have gone

Notes :

1. A = Past Indefinite   B = Present Perfect
    C = Past Perfect   D = Doubtful Past

2. The past tense is formed by adding 'आ' (aa) or या (yaa) to the verb root. The verb root ending
    with a vowel will take the suffix या (yaa); otherwise 'आ' (aa)

आ (Aa)	आया (Aayaa)	सो (So)	सोया (Soyaa)
बैठ (Bytt)	बैठा (Byttaa)	उठ (Utt)	उठा (Uttaa)

III इन शब्दों को सीखिये :

कोशिश*	कोशिश कर
आशा*	आशा कर
मदद*/सहायता*	मदद कर/सहायता कर
माफ़ी*	माफ़ कर
देर*	देर कर
खुशी*	खुश हो
खुश (adjective)	खुश कर
समझ*(N)	समझ
जीवन	जी
सांस*	सांस ले
शायद	अचानक
जल्दी-जल्दी	देर से
अनजाने में	ज़रूर
ज़रूरी	ज़रूरत*

III **Different Past Tense Forms**

A	B	C	D
आया	आया है	आया था	आया होगा
गया	गया है	गया था	गया होगा

The suffixes आ/या (m.s.) will be changed to ए/ये (ye) in masculine plural, ई/यी (ee/yee) in feminine singular and ई/यीं (ee(n)/yee(n)) in feminine plural

आया	आये	आयी	आयीं	Came
aayaa	aaye	aayee	aayee(n)	
सोया	सोये	सोयी	सोयीं	Slept
Soyaa	Soye	Soyee	Soyee(n)	
बैठा	बैठे	बैठी	बैठीं	Sat
Byttaa	Bytte	Byttee	Byttee(n)	
उठा	उठे	उठी	उठीं	Got up
Utta	Utte	Uttee	Uttee(n)	

Laayaa	Laayaa hai	Laayaa thaa	Laayaa hogaa
brought	has brought	had brought	might have brought
Byttaa	Byttaa hai	Bytta thaa	Byttaa hogaa
sat	has sat	had sat	might have sat
Soyaa	Soyaa hai	Soyaa thaa	Soyaa hogaa
slept	has slept	had slept	might have slept

लाया	लाया है	लाया था	लाया होगा
बैठा	बैठा है	बैठा था	बैठा होगा
सोया	सोया है	सोया था	सोया होगा

Lesson 3

I. **Read :**

(A) Hum subah nau baje ghar se nikalthe hai(n)

Hum das baje daftar pahu(n)chthe hai(n)

Humaare dost baarah baje aathe hai(n).

Meree behan kaam karthee hai.

Meree maa(n) school me(n) paḍhaathee hai.

Mere pitaji vyaapaar karthe hai(n).

(B) Tumko/tumne(n) kyaa chaahiye?   **Mujhko/Mujhe kitab chaahiye.**

Hum ko/Hume(n) kuch nahee(n) chaahiye.

Bachcho(n) ko kalam chaahiye   Meree maa(n) ko aaraam chaahiye.

Hume(n) yahaa(n) saaḍhe paa(n)ch baje aanaa chaahiye.

Bachcho(n) ko aatt baje school jaanaa chaahiye.

Mere dost ko Hindi seekhnee chaahiye.

Hume(n) **baraabar** Hindi me(n) bolnaa chaahiye. (continuously)

Aapko aaj humaare dost se milnaa chaahiye.

(see notes below)

(C) **My(n) chhe baje ghar jaa saktaa hoo(n)/saktee hoo(n).**

Kyaa tum Hindi **bol sakte ho?/saktee ho?**

Jee nahee(n), my(n) Hindi nahee(n) bol saktaa hoo(n)/saktee hoo(n).

Lekin meree behne(n) achchee tarah Hindi **bol saktee hai(n).**

Notes:

1. 'Chaahiye' has two usages. It means 'need' and is used as an independent verb. Its second usage is as an auxiliary verb. In both the cases, the subject will take the preposition को (Ko). In the second case 'chaahiye' will be used with the gerund form of the main verb and will mean 'must/ should/ought to'.

पाठ-3

I   **पढ़िये :**

अ)   हम सुबह नौ बजे घर से निकलते हैं।

हम दस बजे दफ़्तर पहुंचते हैं।

हमारे दोस्त बारह बजे आते हैं।

मेरी बहन काम करती है।

मेरी मां स्कूल में पढ़ाती है।

मेरे पिताजी व्यापार करते हैं।

आ)   तुमको/तुम्हें क्या चाहिए?   मुझको/मुझे किताब चाहिए

हमको/हमें कुछ नहीं चाहिए।

बच्चों को कलम चाहिए।   मेरी मां को आराम चाहिए।

हमें यहां साढ़े पांच बजे आना चाहिए।

बच्चों को आठ बजे स्कूल जाना चाहिए।

मेरे दोस्त को हिन्दी सीखनी चाहिए।

हमें **बराबर** हिन्दी में बोलना चाहिए।   (Continuously)

आपको आज हमारे दोस्त से मिलना चाहिए।

इ)   मैं छे बजे घर जा सकता हूं/सकती हूं।

क्या तुम हिन्दी बोल सकते हो/सकती हो?

जी नहीं, मैं हिन्दी नहीं बोल सकता हूं/सकती हूं।

लेकिन मेरी बहनें अच्छी तरह हिन्दी बोल सकती हैं।

Examples:

a)   Bachche Ko Doodh Chaahiye.   The child needs milk.

Mujhe Kitaab Chaahiye.   I need a book.

Meree Behan Ko Ghar Chaahiye. My sister needs a house.

b)   Aapko Hindi me(n) bolnaa chaahiye. You should/ought to speak in Hindi.

Humko Das Baje Daftar Jaanaa Chaahiye. We should/ought to go to office at 10 o'clock.

Mareez ko aaraam karnaa chahiye. The patient should take rest.

Bachchaa tasveer banaa saktaa hai.   Bachche tasveer banaa sakte hai(n).
Bachchee tasveer banaa saktee hai.   Bachchiyaa(n) tasveer banaa saktee hai(n).
Kyaa aap tasveer banaa sakte hai(n)? Jee nahee(n); my(n) tasveer nahee(n) banaa saktaa.
(See notes below)

II. Learn : Karne ke liye = for doing/to do   Paḍhne ke liye = for reading/to read

Khaane ka liye;	Peene ke liye;	Dekhne ke liye,	Likhne ke liye
Jeene ke liye,	Seekhne ke liye,	Khareedne ke liye,	Sun'ne ke liye,
Khelne ke liye,	Milne ke liye	Jaane ke liye	

III. New Words :

Hawaa*	wind	Tez Hawaa	strong wind
Dheemee hawaa	light (soft) wind	Aag*	fire
Dhartee*	earth	Aasmaan	sky
Baadal	cloud	Varshaa*/Barsaat*/Baarish*	rain
Toofaan	typhoon	Aa(n)dhee*	storm/gale
Baaḍh*	flood	Nadee*	river
Jheel*	lake	nahar*	canal
Naalaa	drain	Kuaaa(n)	well
Mausam	weather	Garmee kaa mausam	summer
Tand/Sardee ka mausam	winter	Baarish kaa mausam/ Varshaa kaa mausam	rainy season

---

2. 'सक' (Sak), the auxiliary verb is added to the verb root to indicate ability, the equivalent of which in English is 'Can'. It can be used in all three tenses. Such as:
My(n) Hindi bol saktaa hoo(n). I can speak Hindi.
My(n) Hindi bol sakoo(n)ga. I will be able to speak Hindi.
My(n) Hindi bol sakaa. I was able to speak Hindi.
Meree behan gaa saktee hai. My sister can sing.
Meree behan gaa sakegee. My sister will be able to sing.
Meree behan gaa sakee. My sister was able to sing.

बच्चा तसवीर बना सकता है। बच्चे तसवीर बना सकते हैं।
बच्ची तसवीर बना सकती है। बच्चियां तसवीर बना सकती हैं।
क्या आप तसवीर बना सकते हैं? जी नहीं, मैं तसवीर नहीं बना सकता।

II **सीखिये : करने के लिए, पढ़ने के लिए**

खाने के लिए;	पीने के लिए;	देखने के लिए;	लिखने के लिए;
जीने के लिए;	सीखने के लिए;	**खरीदने के लिए;**	सुनने के लिए;
खेलने के लिए;	मिलने के लिए;	जाने के लिए .	

III **नये शब्द :**

हवा	तेज़ हवा
धीमी हवा	आग
धरती	आसमान
बादल	वर्षा/बरसात/बारिश
तूफ़ान	आंधी
बाढ़	नदी
झील	नहर
नाला	कुआं
मौसम	गरमी का मौसम
ठंड/सरदी का मौसम	बरसात का मौसम/बारिश का मौसम/
	वर्षा का मौसम

CHART

indicating pronouns and changes therein when followed by prepositions :

Pronoun with

	ko	se	me(n)	par	kaa/ke/kee	ne
My(n)	Mujhko/ Mujhe	Mujhse	Mujhme(n)	Mujhpar	Meraa/Mere/ Meree	My(n)ne
Hum	Humko/ Hume(n)	Humse	Hum'me(n)	Humpar	Humaaraa/Humaare/ Humaaree	Humne
Tum	Tumko/ Tumhe(n)	Tumse	Tum'me(n)	Tumpar	Tumhaaraa/Tumhaare Tumhaaree	Tumne
Aap	Aapko	Aapse	Aapme(n)	Aappar	Aap kaa/Aap ke/ Aap kee	Aapne
Vah	Usko/Use	Us'se	Usme(n)	Uspar	Uskaa/Uske/Uskee	Usne
Ve	Unko/ Unhe(n)	Unse	Unme(n)	Unpar	Unkaa/Unke/Unkee	Unho(n)ne
Ye(h)	Isko/Ise	Is'se	Isme(n)	Ispar	Iskaa/Iske/Iskee	Isne
Ye	Inko/ Inhe(n)	Inse	Inme(n)	Inpar	Inkaa/Inke/Inkee	Inho(n)ne
Kaun (Sing.)	Kisko/ Kise	Kis'se	Kisme(n)	Kispar	Kiskaa/Kiske/Kiskee	Kisne
Kaun (Plural)	Kinko/ Kinhe(n)	Kinse	Kinme(n)	Kinpar	Kinkaa/Kinke/ Kinkee	Kinho(n)ne

CHART

indicating pronouns and changes therein when followed by prepositions :

Pronoun with

	को	से	में	पर	का/के/की	ने
मैं	मुझको मुझे	मुझसे	मुझमें	मुझपर	मेरा मेरे मेरी	मैंने
हम	हमको हमें	हमसे	हममें	हमपर	हमारा हमारे हमारी	हमने
तुम	तुमको तुम्हें	तुमसे	तुममें	तुमपर	तुम्हारा तुम्हारे तुम्हारी	तुमने
आप	आपको	आपसे	आपमें	आपपर	आपका आपके आपकी	आपने
वह	उसको उसे	उससे	उसमें	उसपर	उसका उसके उसकी	उसने
वे	उनको उन्हें	उनसे	उनमें	उनपर	उनका उनके उनकी	उन्होंने
यह	इसको इसे	इससे	इसमें	इसपर	इसका इसके इसकी	इसने
ये	इनको इन्हें	इनसे	इनमें	इनपर	इनका इनके इनकी	इन्होंने
कौन (Sing.)	किसको किसे	किससे	किसमें	किसपर	किसका किसके किसकी	किसने
कौन (Pl.)	किनको किन्हें	किनसे	किनमें	किनपर	किनका किनके किनकी	किन्होंने

Lesson-4

I   Read :

A. My(n) Hindi seekhtee hoo(n).   My(n) Hindi samajhna chaahtee hoo(n).

My(n) Hindi khoob bolnaa chaahtee hoo(n).

Tum kya karnaa chaahtee ho?   My(n) Hindi film dekhnaa chaahtee hoo(n).

My(n) apne dosto(n) se Hindi me(n) baatcheet karnaa chaahtee hoo(n).

Hum log hafte me(n) ek bar milte hai(n).

Tab my(n) Hindi kaa istemaal karnaa chaahtee hoo(n).

Aap shaam ko kahaa(n) jaana chaahte hai(n).

My(n) shaam ko pustakaalay jaana chaahtaa hoo(n).

Mere dost bhee mere saath aayenge.

Hum sab vahaa(n) nayee-nayee kitaabe(n) padhnaa chaahte hai(n).

Uske baad hum sab khaane ke liye restaurant jaaye(n)ge.   Kyaa tum bhee chaloge?

Nahee(n), my(n) nahee(n) chal saktaa. kyo(n)ki mujhe aaj jaldee ghar pahu(n)chna

chaahiye. Kuch mehmaan humaare ghar aa rahe hai(n).

Bhayee! Tum saam ko kyaa karnaa chaahoge?

My(n) aaraam karnaa chaahoo(n)ga. **To take rest**

Teek hai; hum kal mile(n)ge.

B.1. I brought a pen.   I have brought a pen.   I had brought a pen.

My(n) kalam laayaa.   My(n) kalam laayaa hoo(n)   **My(n) kalam laayaa thaa.**

She spoke in Hindi   She has spoken in Hindi   She had spoken in Hindi

Vo Hindi me(n) bolee   Vo Hindi me(n) bolee hai   Vo Hindi me(n) bolee thee

We met with our friend   We have met with our friend   We had met with our friend

Hum apne dost se mile.   Hum apne dost se mile hai(n)   Hum apne dost se mile the.

Where did you go?   Where have you gone?   Where had you gone?

Tum kahaa(n) gaye?   Tum kahaa(n) gaye ho?   Tum kahaa(n) gaye the?

पाठ-4

I पढ़िये :

अ) मैं हिन्दी सीखती हूं   मैं हिन्दी समझना चाहती हूं।

मैं हिन्दी खूब बोलना चाहती हूं।

तुम क्या करना चाहती हो?   मैं हिन्दी फ़िल्म देखना चाहती हूं।

मैं अपने दोस्तों से हिन्दी में बातचीत करना चाहती हूं।

हम लोग हफ़्ते में एक बार मिलते हैं।

तब मैं हिन्दी का इस्तेमाल करना चाहती हूं।

आप शाम को कहां जाना चाहते हैं?

मैं शाम को पुस्तकालय जाना चाहता हूं।

मेरे दोस्त भी मेरे साथ आयेंगे।

हम सब वहां नयी-नयी किताबें पढ़ना चाहते हैं।

उसके बाद हम सब खाने के लिए रेस्तोरां जायेंगे; क्या तुम भी चलोगे?

नहीं, मैं नहीं चल सकता। क्योंकि मुझे आज जल्दी घर पहुंचना चाहिए।

कुछ मेहमान हमारे घर आ रहे हैं।

भाई, तुम शाम को क्या करना चाहोगे?

मैं आराम करना चाहूंगा। ठीक है, हम कल मिलेंगे।

आ)

1. मैं कलम लाया।   मैं कलम लाया हूं।   मैं कलम लाया था।

वह हिन्दी में बोली।   वह हिन्दी में बोली है।   वह हिन्दी में बोली थी।

हम अपने दोस्त से मिले।   हम अपने दोस्त से मिले हैं।   हम अपने दोस्त से मिले थे।

तुम कहां गये?   तुम कहां गये हो?   तुम कहां गये थे?

The children sat on the floor	The children have sat on the floor	The children had sat on the floor
Bachche zameen par bytte.	**Bachche zameen par bytte hai(n)**	Bachche zameen par Bytte the

B.2

I read a lesson	I have read a lesson	I had read a lesson
My(n)ne paatt paḍhaa.	My(n)ne paatt paḍhaa hai	**My(n)ne paatt paḍhaa thaa.**
I read the book	I have read the book	I had read the book
My(n)ne kitaab paḍhee	My(n)ne kitaab paḍhee hai	My(n)ne kitaab paḍhee thee
She wrote a letter	She has written a letter	She had written a letter
Usne patra likhaa	Usne patra likhaa hai	Usne patra likha thaa
Usne chitthee likhee	Usne chitthee likhee hai	Usne chitthee likhee thee.
Asha and her sister bought a pen.	Asha and her sister have bought a pen	Asha and her sister had bought a pen
Asha aur uskee behan ne ek kalam khareedee.	Asha aur uskee behan ne ek kalam khareedee Hai.	Asha aur uskee behan ne ek kalam khareedee thee.

II. Learn : Numbers 31-60

31-40

Ikthees	Baththees	Tai(n)thees	Chau(n)thees	Py(n)thees
Chaththees	Sai(n)thees	Aḍthees	Unthaaless	Chaalees

41-50

Ikthaalees	Bayaalees	Tai(n)thaalees	Chavaalees	Py(n)thaalees
Chhiyaalees	Sai(n)thaalees	Aḍthaalees	Unchaas	Pachaas

51-60

Ikyaavan	Baavan	Tirpan	Chauvan	Pachpan
Chhappan	Satthaavan	Attaavan	Unsatt	Saatt

Color   Rang

Laal	red	Kaalaa	black	Safed	white	Peelaa	yellow
Neelaa	blue	Bhooraa	brown	Bynganee	purple	Haraa	green

बच्चे ज़मीन पर बैठे।   बच्चे ज़मीन पर बैठे हैं।   बच्चे ज़मीन पर बैठे थे

2. मैंने पाठ पढ़ा।   मैंने पाठ पढ़ा है।   मैंने पाठ पढ़ा था।

मैंने किताब पढ़ी।   मैंने किताब पढ़ी है।   मैंने किताब पढ़ी थी।

उसने पत्र लिखा।   उसने पत्र लिखा है।   उसने पत्र लिखा था।

उसने चिट्ठी लिखी।   उसने चिट्ठी लिखी है।   उसने चिट्ठी लिखी थी।

आशा और उसकी बहन ने एक कलम खरीदी।

आशा और उसकी बहन ने एक कलम खरीदी है।

आशा और उसकी बहन ने एक कलम खरीदी थी।

II सीखिये :

संख्याएँ 31–60

31–40

इकतीस	बत्तीस	तैंतीस	चौंतीस	पैंतीस
छत्तीस	सैंतीस	अड़तीस	उनतालीस	चालीस

41–50

इकतालीस	बयालीस	तैंतालीस	चवालीस	पैंतालीस
छियालीस	सैंतालीस	अड़तालीस	उनचास	पचास

51–60

इक्यावन	बावन	तिरपन	चौवन	पचपन
छप्पन	**सत्तावन**	**अट्ठावन**	उनसठ	साठ

रंग

लाल	काला	सफ़ेद	पीला	नीला	भूरा	**बैंगनी**	हरा

Note : Learn the use of transitive verbs in past tense:

1. When a transitive verb is used in past tense, post-position 'ne' (ने) should be added to the subject.

    My(n)ne chaaval khaayaa.   I ate rice.
    मैंने चावल खाया।

2. The verb generally agrees with the subject in gender and number; but in the case of the subject having the post-position 'ne' (ने) , the verb agrees with the object in gender and number.

    Joseph ne rotee khaayee.   Joseph ate bread.
    जोसफ ने रोटी खायी।

    Reeta ne aam khaayaa.   Rita ate mango.
    रीता ने आम खाया।

3. When the object is followed by post-position 'ko' (को) then the verb remains in masculine singular.

    Mere bhaayee ne yek billee paalee.   My brother raised a cat.
    मेरे भाई ने एक बिल्ली पाली।

    Meree behan ne bhee yek billee ko paalaa.   My sister also raised a cat.
    मेरी बहन ने भी एक बिल्ली को पाला।

4. When the object is understood - not given explicitly - then also the verb remains in masculine singular.

Bachche ne khaayaa.　　　　बच्चे ने खाया।

Bachcho(n) ne khaayaa.　　बच्चों ने खाया।

Bachchee ne khaayaa　　　बच्ची ने खाया।

Bachchiyo(n) ne khaayaa.　बच्चियों ने खाया।
(The child/children ate.)

5.　Since 'ne' (ने) is a post-position, the nouns and pronouns when followed by 'Ne' are subjected to usual changes.

Ladke ne kitaab padhee.　　The boy read a book.
लड़के ने किताब पढ़ी।

Ladko(n) ne tasveer banaayee. The boys drew a picture.
लड़कों ने तसवीर बनायी।

(Vo + ne)　Usne chitthee likhee.　　　　He/She wrote a letter.
　　　　　उसने चिट्ठी लिखी।

(Ye(h) + ne)　Isne kaam kiyaa.　　　　This (person) did work.
　　　　　इसने काम किया।

(Kaun + ne)　Kisne ghar banaaya?　　Who built the house?
(singular)　किसने घर बनाया?

　Ve, Ye and Kaun (pl.) will change to Unho(n), Inho(n) and Kinho(n) respectively.
　Unho(n)ne Dookaan khareedee.　　They bought a store.
　उन्होंने दूकान खरीदी।

Inho(n)ne kitaab paḍhee. इन्होंने किताब पढ़ी।	Thsee (people) read a book.
Kinho(n)ne kapḍe khareede? किन्होंने कपड़े खरीदे?	Who bought clothes?

6. The above rules will apply not only in the past indefinite, but also in the present perfect, past perfect and doubtful past.

a.
Hum ne rotee khaayee	We ate bread.
Hum ne rotee khaayee hai.	We have eaten bread.
Hum ne rotee khaayee thee.	We had eaten bread.
Hum ne rotee khaayee hogee.	We might have eaten bread.

b.
My(n)ne chaai pee	I drank tea.
My(n)ne chaai pee hai	I have drunk tea.
My(n)ne chaai pee thee	I had drunk tea.
My(n)ne chaai pee hogee	I might have drunk tea.

c.
Usne achchhaa kaam kiyaa.	**He did good work.**
Usne achchhaa kaam kiyaa hai.	**He has done good work.**
Usne achchhaa kaam kiyaa tha.	**He had done good work.**
Usne achchhaa kaam kiyaa hogaa.	**He might have done good work.**

7. The following transitive verbs are exempted from the above rules. They will be used as intransitive verbs.

Laa (ला) bring	Bol (बोल) speak
Bhool (भूल) forget	Mil (मिल) meet

Bachchaa kitaab laayaa.   The child brought a book.
बच्चा किताब लाया।

Meree behan mujh se bolee. My sister spoke to me.
मेरी बहन मुझसे बोली।

Vo apnee thailee bhoolaa.   He forgot his bag
वह अपनी थैली भूला। (usually used as bhool gayaa भूल गया)

My(n) apne dost se milaa.   I met with my friend.
मैं अपने दोस्त से मिला।

Lesson-5

I. Read :

Naye Shabd (New Words)

Relationship (Rishta)

Ancestors	Baap-Daadaa		
Father	Baap; Pithaa	Mother	Maa(n); Maathaa
Son	Betaa	Daughter	Betee
Grandson	Pothaa	Grand daughter	Pothee
Grand father	Daadaa(paternal)		Naanaa (maternal)
Grand mother	Daadee(paternal)		Naanee (maternal)
Uncle	Chaachaa (father's brother)	Maamaa	Mother's brother
Brother	Bhaayee/Bhaiyaa	Sister	Behan
Brother's wife	Bhaabhee	Sister's husband	Behnoyee
Brother's son	Bhatheejaa	Brother's daughter	Bhatheejee
Sister's son	Bhaa(n)jaa	Sister's daughter	Bhaa(n)jee
Husband	Pathi	Wife	Patnee/Stree
Son-in-law	Daamaad	Daughter-in-law	Bahoo
Mother-in-law	Saas	Father-in-law	Sasur
Aunt (father's sister)	Buaa	Mother's sister	Mausee
Guest	Mehmaan	Host	Mezbaan
Parents	Maa(n)-Baap		

II. Sentences (Vaakya) :

A) My(n) yahaa(n) chhe baje aayaa.   Hum sab bhee chhe baje pahu(n)che.

My(n)ne ek sundar chitra banaayaa.

My(n)ne ek sundar tasveer banaayee.

पाठ-5

I **पढ़िये : नये शब्द**

रिश्ता

बाप-दादा

बाप/पिता	मां/माता
बेटा	बेटी
पोता	पोती
दादा	दादी
नाना	नानी
चाचा	मामा
भाई/भैया	भाभी
बहन	बहनोई
भतीजा	भतीजी
भांजा	भांजी
पति	पत्नी/स्त्री
दामाद	बहू
सास	ससुर
बुआ	मौसी
मेहमान	मेज़बान

मां-बाप

II **वाक्य :**

अ) मैं यहां छे बजे आया।   हम सब भी छे बजे पहुंचे।

मैंने एक सुन्दर चित्र बनाया।   मैंने एक सुन्दर तसवीर बनायी।

Hum ne apnaa paatt paḍhaa. Humne apnee kitaab paḍhee.

Humaare dosto(n) ne apnee maa(n) ko patra likhaa.

Meree behno(n) ne do-teen patra likhe.

Mere dost ke pitaajee ne apnee betee ko chitthee likhee.

Bhaayee, tumne kal kitnee chitthiyaa(n) likhee(n)?

My(n)ne kal nahee(n), parso(n) ek chitthee likhee.

bachche ne sabere doodh piyaa.

Bachcho(n) ne apne school kaa kaam kiyaa.

Humaaree behan ne apne bhaayee ke liye kapḍaa khareedaa.

Maa(n) ne bachno(n) ke liye kameez khareedee.

Behan, tum kal kitne baje ghar gayee(n)?

My(n) raat ko nau baje ghar gayee.

Meraa dost bhee mere saath thaa.

Usne mujhe ghar pahu(n)chaaya aur baad me(n) apne ghar gayaa.

Ve log sabere ki gaaḍee se gaa(n)v gaye.

Ve vahaa(n) ek meheena rahe(n)ge aur kuchh kaam kare(n)ge.

My(n) bhee baad me(n) apne dosto(n) ke saath gaa(n)v jaaoo(n)gaa.

B. Use of 'SAK' (can; will be able to; was able to)

Review

1. **Meraa bhaaye Hindi bol saktaa hai.**

   Mere bachche bhee Hindi bol sakte hai(n).

   Humaaree behan Hindi likh saktee hai.

   Humaaree behne(n) Hindi geet gaa saktee hai(n).

2. Kya tum Hindi me(n) bol sakoge?

   Jee nahee(n); My(n) ek saal ke baad Hindi me(n) bol sakoo(n)gaa.

   Meree sahelee Hindi me(n) kavita likh sakegee.

   Meree maa(n) aur unkee saheliyaa(n) Hindi geet gaa sake(n)gee.

3. Bchchaa aaraam se so sakaa.   Ve log aaraam kar sake

   Vo laḍkee pichle saal Bhaarat jaa Sakee.

   Meree saheliyaa(n) imthahaan de sakee(n)   **imthahaan = Examination**

हमने अपना पाठ पढ़ा।   हमने अपनी किताब पढ़ी।

हमारे दोस्तों ने अपनी मां को पत्र लिखा।

मेरी बहनों ने दो-तीन पत्र लिखे।

मेरे दोस्त के पिताजी ने अपनी बेटी को चिट्ठी लिखी।

भाई, तुमने कल कितनी चिट्ठियां लिखीं?

मैंने कल नहीं, परसों एक चिट्ठी लिखी।

बच्चे ने सबेरे दूध पिया।

बच्चों ने अपने स्कूल का काम किया।

हमारी बहन ने अपने भाई के लिए कपड़ा खरीदा।

मां ने बच्चों के लिए कमीज़ खरीदी।

बहन, तुम कल कितने बजे घर गयीं?

मैं रात को नौ बजे घर गयी।

मेरा दोस्त भी मेरे साथ था।

उसने मुझे घर पहुंचाया और बाद में अपने घर गया।

वे लोग सबेरे की गाड़ी से गांव गये। वे वहां एक महीना रहेंगे और कुछ काम करेंगे।

मैं भी बाद में अपने दोस्तों के साथ गांव जाऊंगा।

आ) Use of सक :

i) मेरा भाई हिन्दी बोल सकता है।   मेरे बच्चे भी हिन्दी बोल सकते हैं।

    हमारी बहन हिन्दी लिख सकती है।   हमारी बहनें हिन्दी गीत गा सकती हैं।

ii) क्या तुम हिन्दी में बोल सकोगे?   जी नहीं, मैं एक साल के बाद हिन्दी में बोल सकूंगा।

    मेरी सहेली हिन्दी में कविता लिख सकेगी।   मेरी मां और उनकी सहेलियां हिन्दी गीत गा सकेंगी।

iii) बच्चा आराम से सो सका।   वे लोग आराम कर सके।

    वह लड़की पिछले साल भारत जा सकी।   मेरी सहेलियां **इम्तहान** दे सकीं।

C) Use of 'CHUK'; This subsidiary verb indicates the completion of some work and will be added to a main root verb–without any change.

Bachchaa sabak likh chukaa

Bchche khel chuke.

Bachchee ghar ka kaam kar chukee.

Bachchiyaa(n) gaanaa seekh chukee(n)

III. Learn :

Paav ¼	Aadhaa ½	Paun $^3/_4$	Ek (yek) one
Savaa yek	$1^1/_4$ (Savaa is also used for $1^1/_4$)		
Deḍh $1^1/_2$	Paune do $1^3/_4$		Do two
Savaa do $2^1/_4$	Dhaayee/Aḍhaayee 2½	Paune teen $2^3/_4$	Teen three
Savaa teen $3^1/_4$	Saaḍhe teen $3^1/_2$	Paune chaar $3^3/_4$	Chaar four
Savaa chaar $4^1/_4$	Saaḍhe chaar $4^1/_2$	Paune paa(n)ch $4^3/_4$	Paa(n)ch five

IV. Past Tense—Intransitive & Transitive Verbs : (Review)

My(n) ṣaam ko ghar gayaa.

Mere pitajee chhae baje ghar aaye.

Meree mataajee ne hum sabke liye khaanaa banaayaa.

My(n)ne aatt baje khaanaa khaayaa.

Mere bhaavee ne rotee khaayee.

Meree behno(n) ne chaaval khaayaa.

Aapke laḍke saath baje kahaa(n) gaye?

Mere laḍke saath baje mandir gaye.

Uskaa laḍkaa sabere chhe baje uttaa.

Usne aadhaa ghantaa Hindi kitaab paḍhee.

My(n)ne sabere naaṣtha kiyaa.

Naaṣthe me(n) my(n)ne rotee khaayee aur santare kaa ras piyaa.

Bachcho(n) ne ṣhaam ko gaanaa seekhaa.

Kayee ladkiyo(n) ne bhee gaanaa seekhaa.

Meree maa(n) ne school me(n) bachcho(n) ko gaanaa sikhaayaa.

इ) Use of चुक

बच्चा सबक लिख चुका।   बच्चे खेल चुके।

बच्ची घर का काम कर चुकी।   बच्चियां गाना सीख चुकीं।

III सीखिये :

पाव $\frac{1}{4}$	आधा $\frac{1}{2}$	पौन $\frac{3}{4}$	एक 1
सवा एक (सवा)$1\frac{1}{4}$	डेढ़ $1\frac{1}{2}$	पौने दो $1\frac{3}{3}$	दो 2
सवा दो $2\frac{1}{4}$	ढाई/अढ़ाई $2\frac{1}{2}$	पौने तीन $2\frac{3}{4}$	तीन 3
सवा तीन $3\frac{1}{4}$	साढ़े तीन $3\frac{1}{2}$	पौने चार $3\frac{3}{4}$	चार 4
सवा चार $4\frac{1}{4}$	साढ़े चार $4\frac{1}{2}$	पौने पांच $4\frac{3}{4}$	पांच 5

IV Past Tense—Intransitive & Transitive Verbs : Review

मैं शाम को घर गया।   मेरे पिताजी छे बजे घर आये।

मेरी माताजी ने हम सबके लिए खाना बनाया।

मैंने आठ बजे खाना खाया।   मेरे भाई ने रोटी खायी।

मेरी बहनों ने चावल खाया।   आपके लड़के सात बजे कहां गये?

मेरे लड़के सात बजे मंदिर गये।

उसका लड़का सबेरे छे बजे उठा।

उसने आधा घंटा हिन्दी किताब पढ़ी।

मैंने सबेरे नाश्ता किया।

नाश्ते में मैंने रोटी खायी और संतरे का रस पिया।

बच्चों ने शाम को गाना सीखा।

कई लड़कियों ने भी गाना सीखा।

मेरी मां ने स्कूल में बच्चों को गाना सिखाया।

Lesson-6

I. Read :

Naye Shabd (New Words)

Nouns :

Chaa(n)d	moon	Chaa(n)dnee*	moonlight
Sooraj	sun	Dhoop*	(direct) sunlight
Loo*	hot wind	Taaraa	star
Indra Dhanush	rainbow	Bijlee*	lightning/thunder/electricity
Baadal	cloud	Barsaat*/Baarish*/Varshaa*	rain
Diṣaa*	direction	Sawaal/Praṣna	question
Jawaab/Uttar	answer/reply	Patra/Khat/Chitthee*	letter

Verbs :

Bah	flow	Pahu(n)ch	reach	Chamak	Shine
Kaḍak	thundering				
Baras (paanee baras) rain		Khaa eat	Khilaa	feed	Dekh see
Dikhaa show	So	sleep	Sulaa	to cause to sleep	

II. Answer the following :

Aapko kyaa chaahiye?   Tumhare dost ko kyaa chaahiye?

Tumko kitne baje daftar jaanaa chaahiye?   Bachcho(n) ko kahaa(n) khelnaa chaahiye?

Kyaa aap Hindi bol saktee hai(n)?   Tum yahaa(n) kab aa saktee ho?

Kyaa tumhaaraa chotaa bhayee Hindi seekh saktaa hai? Kyaa vo bachchee gaa saktee hai?

Yahaa(n) kitne log Hindi seekh rahe hai(n)?   Aap mujhse kab mile(n)ge?

Uskee behan kal kahaa(n) se aa rahee thee? Ve log agle hafte kahaa(n) jaaye(n)ge?

पाठ-6

I   पढ़िये : नये शब्द

Nouns

चांद	चांदनी
सूरज	धूप
लू	तारा
इन्द्रधनुष	बिजली
बादल	बरसात/बारिश/वर्षा
दिशा	सवाल/प्रश्न
जवाब/उत्तर	पत्र/खत/चिट्ठी

Verbs

बह	पहुंच	चमक	कड़क
बरस (पानी बरस)		खा	खिला
देख		दिखा	
सो		सुला	

II   उत्तर दीजिये :

आपको क्या चाहिए?   तुम्हारे दोस्त को क्या चाहिए?

तुमको कितने बजे दफ़्तर जाना चाहिए?

बच्चों को कहां खेलना चाहिए?

क्या आप हिन्दी बोल सकती हैं?   तुम यहां कब आ सकती हो?

क्या तुम्हारा छोटा भाई हिन्दी सीख सकता है?   क्या वह बच्ची गा सकती है?

यहां कितने लोग हिन्दी सीख रहे हैं?   आप मुझसे कब मिलेंगे?

उसकी बहन कल कहां से आ रही थी?   वे लोग अगले हफ़्ते कहां जायेंगे?

Tum kal kahaa(n) gayee(n)?

Kyaa tumhaaree saheliyaa(n) bhee tumhaare saath thee(n)?

Aapne sabere kyaa khaayaa?

Usne dookaan me(n) kitne phal khareede?

III Learn:

Numbers 61-80

61-70

| Iksatt | **Baasatt** | Tirsatt | Chau(n)satt | Py(n)satt |
| Chiyaasatt | Sadsatt | Adsatt | Unhattar | Sattar |

71-80

| Ikhattar | Bahattar | Tihattar | Chauhattar | Pachhattar |
| Chihattar | Sathattar | Atthattar | Unnaasee | Assee |

CHART

Verbs in Different Tenses (Review)

Present	Present Continuous	Future	Past	Past Continuous
Singular--Masculine				
My(n) Aathaa hoo(n)	Aa rahaa hoo(n)	Aaoongaa	Aayaa	Aa rahaa thaa
Tum Aathe Ho	Aa rahe ho	Aaoge	Aaye	Aa rahe the
Vo Ye(h) Kaun } Aathaa hai	Aa rahaa hai	Aayegaa	Aayaa	Aa rahaa thaa
Plural--Masculine				
Hum Aap Ve Ye Kaun } Aathe hai(n)	Aa rahe hai(n)	Aayenge	Aaye	Aa rahe the

तुम कल कहां गयीं?

क्या तुम्हारी सहेलियां भी तुम्हारे साथ थीं?

आपने सबेरे क्या खाया?

उसने दूकान में कितने फल खरीदे?

III **संख्याएँ 61-80**

61-70

इकसठ	बासठ	तिरसठ	चौंसठ	पैंसठ
छियासठ	सड़सठ	अड़सठ	उनहत्तर	सत्तर

71-80

इकहत्तर	बहत्तर	तिहत्तर	चौहत्तर	पचहत्तर
छिहत्तर	सतहत्तर	अठहत्तर	उन्नासी	अस्सी

चार्ट (सारणी)
Verbs in Different Tenses (Review)

Present	Present Continuous	Future	Past	Past Continuous
Singular--Masculine				
मैं आता हूं	आ रहा हूं	आऊंगा	आया	आ रहा था
तुम आते हो	आ रहे हो	आओगे	आये	आ रहे थे
वह यह } आता है कौन	आ रहा है	आयेगा	आया	आ रहा था
Plural-Masculine				
हम आप वे } आते हैं ये कौन	आ रहे हैं	आयेंगे	आये	आ रहे थे

Past Tense - Intransitive (Masculine)

I.
Intransitive (Masculine)	Transitive Verbs
Bachchaa soyaa	Ashok ne rotee khaayee
Bachche soye	Ashok ne rotiyaa(n) khaayee(n)
Bachchee soyee	Meera ne doodh piyaa
Bachchiyaa(n) soyee(n)	Meera ne chaai pee

II.

Intransitive (Masculine)

Verb	Past	Present Perfect	Past Perfect	Doubtful Past
My(n)	aayaa	aayaa hoo(n)	aayaa thaa	aayaa hoongaa
Tum	aaye	aaye ho	aaye the	aaye hoge
Vo Ye(h) Kaun	aayaa	aayaa hai	aayaa thaa	aayaa hogaa
Hum Aap Ve Ye Kaun	aaye	aaye hai(n)	aaye the	aaye honge

Transitive

	Present Perfect	Past Perfect	Doubtful Past
My(n)ne Chaaval Khaayaa	Khaayaa hai	Khaayaa thaa	Khaayaa hoga
Bachcho(n) ne aam khaayaa	khaayaa hai	khaayaa thaa	khaayaa hogaa
Mere bhaayee ne kithaab khareedee	khareedee hai	khareedee thee	khareedee hogee
Meree behan ne ghar khareedaa	khareedaa hai	khareedaa thaa	khareedaa hogaa

Past Tense - Intransitive (Masculine)

Transitive Verbs

I   बच्चा सोया   अशोक ने रोटी खायी

     बच्चे सोये   अशोक ने रोटियां खायीं

     बच्ची सोयी   मीरा ने दूध पिया

     बच्चियां सोयीं   मीरा ने चाय पी

II.   Verb

Past	Present Perfect	Past Perfect	Doubtful Past
Intransitive (Masculine)			
मैं आया	आया हूं	आया था	आया हूंगा
तुम आये	आये हो	आये थे	आये होगे
वह यह कौन } आया	आया है	आया था	आया होगा
हम आप वे ये कौन } आये	आये हैं	आये थे	आये होंगे

Transitive

Past	Present Perfect	Past Perfect	Doubtful Past
मैंने चावल खाया	खाया है	खाया था	खाया होगा
बच्चों ने आम खाया	खाया है	खाया था	खाया होगा
मेरे भाई ने किताब खरीदी	खरीदी है	खरीदी थी	खरीदी होगी
मेरी बहन ने घर खरीदा	खरीदा है	खरीदा था	खरीदा होगा

Lesson - 7

I. **Words :**

*a.

Gaai*	Cow	Bhai(n)s*	buffalo	Ghoḍaa	horse		
Bakree*	goat	Haathee	elephant	Oo(n)t	camel	Hiran	deer
Kuththaa	dog	Billee*	cat	Choohaa	mouse	Choojaa	chicken
Oolloo	owl	Siyaar	jackal	Lomḍee	fox		

b.

Pahlaa	Doosraa	Teesraa	Chauthaa	Paa(n)chvaa(n)
first	second	third	fourth	fifth
Chattaa	Saatvaa(n)	Aattvaa(n)	Navaa(n)	Dasvaa(n)
sixth	seventh	eighth	ninth	tenth

c.

Dono(n)	Teeno(n)	Chaaro(n)	Paa(n)cho(n)	Chhaho(n)
both	all three	all four	all five	all six
Saato(n)	Aatto(n)	Navo(n)	Daso(n)	
all seven	all eight	all nine	all ten	

d.

Kee tarah	like	Kee taraf/kee ore	toward
ke jaise	like	Ke Baraabar	equal to
Ke alaava	in addition	ke sivaa/sivaay	except
ke binaa	without		

(These are used with nouns and pronouns)

II. **Please answer :**

Ghar ke peeche kyaa hai?

Saamne kaun khel rahaa hai?

---

* A few words have been repeated for the purpose of review

पाठ-7

I **शब्द :**

a. | गाय | भैंस | घोड़ा |
बकरी	हाथी	ऊंट
हिरन	कुत्ता	बिल्ली
चूहा	चूजा	उल्लू
सियार	लोमड़ी	

b. | पहला | दूसरा | तीसरा |
चौथा	पांचवां	छठा
सातवां	आठवां	नवां
दसवां		

c. | दोनों | तीनों | चारों |
   | पांचों | छहों | सातों |
   | आठों | ननों | दसों |

d. | की तरह | की तरफ़/की ओर |
के जैसे	के बराबर
के अलावा	के सिवा/सिवाय
के बिना	

II **जवाब दीजिये :**

घर के पीछे क्या है?
सामने कौन खेल रहा है?

Aap sabere kahaa(n) **tahalthe hai(n)**?   roam/stroll/walk

Bachchaa kiske saath school jaa rahaa hai?

Aapke bachche kis bhaashaa me(n) bolthe hai(n)?

Ve log kahaa(n) jaa rahe hai(n)?

Tum log yahaa(n) kyaa karthe ho?

Tumhaare dosto(n) ko kyaa chaahiye?

Bachcho(n) ko kitne baje school jaanaa chaahiye?

Kyaa tum Hindi bol sakte ho?

Kyaa tumhaare darje ke **vidyaarthee** Hindi me(n) likh sakte hai(n)?   student

Kyaa aap roz Hindi kakshaa me(n) aa sakte hai(n)?

Aap Hindi seekhkar kyaa kare(n)ge?

Hum log pustakaalaya jaakar kyaa kare(n)ge?

Vah ladkee dookaan me(n) kyaa karegee?

Tumne aaj kyaa khaayaa?

Aapne yahaa(n) kyaa seekhaa?

Aapke dosto(n) ne yah kitaab kahaa(n) khareedee?

III. Use of Vaalaa (Vaale/Vaalee) as Suffix to a Noun/Verb

a. Indicates ownership/seller :   Gharvaalaa   Gaadeevaalaa

                                        Pysevaalaa   Doodhvaalaa

                                        Mittaayeevaalaa   Khilaunevaalaa

b. Indicates place that one belongs to : Dilleevaalaa   Bombayvaalaa

                                        Dakshinvaalaa   Uttarvaalaa

                                        Gaa(n)v'vaalaa   Saharvaalaa

c. Indicates the doer of some action : Khaanevaalaa   Sonevaalaa

                                        Peenevaalaa   Ronevaalaa

                                        Jaanevaalaa   Bechnevaalaa

---

Note : The suffix **Vaalaa** changes to **Vaale** and **Vaalee** in masculine plural and feminine singular & plural respectively.

आप सबेरे कहां **टहलते हैं**?

बच्चा किसके साथ स्कूल जा रहा है?

आपके बच्चे किस भाषा में बोलते हैं?

वे लोग कहां जा रहे हैं?

तुम लोग यहां क्या करते हो?

तुम्हारे दोस्तों को क्या चाहिए?

बच्चों को कितने बजे स्कूल जाना चाहिए?

क्या तुम हिन्दी बोल सकते हो?

क्या तुम्हारे दर्जे के विद्यार्थी हिन्दी में लिख सकते हैं?

क्या आप रोज़ हिन्दी कक्षा में आ सकते हैं?

आप हिन्दी सीखकर क्या करेंगे?

हम लोग पुस्तकालय जाकर क्या करेंगे?

वह लड़की दूकान में क्या करेगी?

तुमने आज क्या खाया?

आपने यहां क्या सीखा?

आपके दोस्तों ने यह किताब कहां खरीदी?

III   Use of वाला (वाले/वाली) as suffix to a noun/verb

a.	Indicates ownership/ seller :	घरवाला	गाड़ीवाला
		पैसेवाला	दूधवाला
		मिठाईवाला	खिलौनेवाला

b.	Indicates place that one belongs to :	दिल्लीवाला	बंबईवाला
		दक्षिणवाला	उत्तरवाला
		गांववाला	शहरवाला

c.	Indicates the doer of some action :	खानेवाला	सोनेवाला
		पीनेवाला	रोनेवाला
		जानेवाला	बेचनेवाला

IV. Read/Learn the following sentenses :

Meree behan khoob Hindi bolthee hai.

My(n) bhee uski tarah Hindi bolnaa chaahthee hoo(n).

Mere bhaayee bhee Hindi bolnaa chaahthe hai(n).

Aap log chhuttiyo(n) me(n) kahaa(n) jaanaa chaahthe hai(n)?

Hum log chhuttiyo(n) me(n) Florida jaanaa chaahthe hai(n).

Meree maa(n) aur buvaa shaam ko mandir jaanaa chaahthee hai(n).

My(n) bhee unke saath jaaoongee.

Mujhe ek achchaa ghar chaahiye.

Bachcho(n) ko khilaune chaahiye.

Mere dosto(n) ko ek gaadee chaahiye.

Aapko kal sabere sahar jaanaa chaahiye.

Tumko ghar ka kaam karnaa chaahiye.

Bachcho(n) ko ghar ke baahar nahee(n) khelnaa chaahiye.

Hume(n) pustakaalaya me(n) kuch puraanee kitabe(n) dhco(n)dhnee chaahiye.

(to search)

Aap yahaa(n) har hafte aa saktee hai(n) aur Hindi seekh saktee hai(n).

Kyaa my(n) bhee aa saktee hoo(n)? Kyo(n) nahee(n), aap bhee zaroor aa saktee hai(n).

Kyaa ve chaai pee sakte hai(n)?

Jee nahee(n); ve chaai nahee(n), coffee pee sakte hai(n).

IV **इन वाक्यों को पढ़िये/सीखिये :**

मेरी बहन खूब हिन्दी बोलती है।

मैं भी **उसकी तरह** हिन्दी बोलना चाहती हूं।

मेरे भाई भी हिन्दी बोलना चाहते हैं।

आप लोग छुट्टियों में कहां जाना चाहते हैं?

हम लोग छुट्टियों में फ़्लारिडा जाना चाहते हैं।

मेरी मां और बुआ शाम को मंदिर जाना चाहती हैं।

मैं भी उनके साथ जाऊंगी।

मुझे एक अच्छा घर चाहिए।

बच्चों को खिलौने चाहिए।

मेरे दोस्तों को एक गाड़ी चाहिए।

आपको कल सबेरे शहर जाना चाहिए।

तुमको घर का काम करना चाहिए।

बच्चों को घर के बाहर नहीं खेलना चाहिए।

हमें पुस्तकालय में कुछ पुरानी किताबें ढूंढ़नी चाहिए।

आप यहां हर हफ़्ते आ सकती हैं और हिन्दी सीख सकती हैं।

क्या मैं भी आ सकती हूं?

क्यों नहीं, आप भी ज़रूर आ सकती हैं।

क्या वे चाय पी सकते हैं?

जी नहीं, वे चाय नहीं, कॉफ़ी पी सकते हैं।

Lesson - 8

I. Naye Shabd (New Words) :

Khiḍkee*	window	Darvaazaa	door	Thaalaa	lock
Chaabee*	key	Baraamdaa	Verandah (large open area inside the house)		
Byttak khaanaa	living room	Rasoyee ghar	kitchen	Snaan ghar	bathroom
Saamaan ghar	store room	Sone ka kamraa (ṣayan kaksh)		bed room	

Kamal/Pankaj	lotus	Gulaab	rose	Mallika	jasmine
Kachchaa	unripe/raw	Pakkaa	ripe/well built	Pakaa	ripe (fruit) /Cooked

Taazaa	fresh	Baasee	rotten	khaas/viṣesh special
Maamoolee	ordinary			
Chun	to pick/elect			
Gin	to count	Bun	to weave	
Sun	to hear/listen	Sunvaayee	hearing of a case	
Chunaav	election			
Ginthee	calculation	Bunaayee	weaving	
Dho	to wash			
Dhulaayee	cleaning/washing			
Ro	to cry			
Rulaayee	crying			
Paḍh	to study/to read			
Paḍhaayee	reading/studying			
Ha(n)s	to laugh			
Ha(n)see	laughter			

II. Please answer :

Aapne ye(h) kithaab kahaa(n) khareedee?

Aapke dost ne sabere kyaa piyaa?

Tumhaare bhaaiyo(n) aur behno(n) ne ṣahar me(n) kyaa/kyaa dekhaa?

Uskee maataajee ne tumko kyaa diyaa?

पाठ-8

I   **नये शब्द :**

खिड़की	दरवाज़ा	ताला
चाबी	बरामदा	
बैठक खाना	रसोई घर	स्नान घर
सामान घर	सोने का कमरा (शयन कक्ष)	
कमल/पंकज	गुलाब	मल्लिका
कच्चा	पक्का	पका
ताज़ा	बासी	खास/विशेष
मामूली	बुन	
चुन	बुनाई	
गिन	सुनवाई	
सुन		
चुनाव		
गिनती		
धो		
धुलाई		
रो		
रुलाई		
पढ़		
पढ़ाई		
हंस		
हंसी		

उत्तर दीजिये :

आपने यह किताब कहां खरीदी?

आपके दोस्त ने सबेरे क्या किया?

तुम्हारे भाइयों और बहनों ने शहर में क्या क्या-क्या देखा?

उसकी माताजी ने तुमको क्या दिया

Aap sabere kahaa(n) gayee(n)?

Tumhaaree behan ṣahar se kyaa laayee?

Tumhaaree behan ne kahaa(n) sangeet seekhaa?

Aapne yah gaanaa kahaa(n) sunaa?

Aapke ghar se daftar kitnee door hai?

Aap daftar kyse jaathee hai(n)?

Aap daftar jaakar kyaa karthee hai(n)?

Aap kitne baje se kitne baje tak daftar me(n) rahthee hai(n)?

Aap daftar me(n) kitne ghante kaam karthee hai(n)?

Tum kitne din ke liye chhuttee par jaaoge?

Tum chhuttiyo(n) me(n) kyaa karoge?

Aap Hindi seekhkar kyaa kare(n)gee?

Aap pustakaalay jaakar kyaa kare(n)ge?

Aajkal mausam kysaa hai?

Kyaa aapko ye(h) mausam pasand hai?

Mittaayeevaalaa kyaa karthaa hai?

Kyaa tumko mittaayee pasand hai?

III. Learn :

Tum Hindi seekhkar kyaa karogee?

My(n) Hindi seekhkar Bharat jaaoo(n)gee.

Mera bhaayee ṣaam ko ghar jaakar bhojan karegaa.

Meree maa(n) khaanaa banaakar bachcho(n) ko khilaathee hai.

Mere pita jee khaanaa khaakar ṣahar jaate hai(n).

Vo apnaa kaam karke ghar gayaa.

Mere baḍe bhaayee kasrat karke laute.

Learn these forms :

Seekhkar = having leanrt

Jaakar = having gone

Banaakar = having made/prepared

आप सबेरे कहां गयीं?

तुम्हारी बहन शहर से क्या लायी?

तुम्हारी बहन ने कहां संगीत सीखा?

आपने यह गाना कहां सुना?

आपके घर से दफ़्तर कितनी दूर है?

आप दफ़्तर कैसे जाती हैं?

आप दफ़्तर जाकर क्या करती हैं?

आप कितने बजे से कितने बजे तक दफ़्तर में रहती हैं?

आप दफ़्तर में कितने घंटे काम करती हैं?

तुम कितने दिन के लिए छुट्टी पर जाओगे?

तुम छुट्टियों में क्या करोगे?

आप हिन्दी सीखकर क्या करेंगी?

आप पुस्तकालय जाकर क्या करेंगे?

आजकल मौसम कैसा है?

क्या आपको यह मौसम पसंद है?

मिठाईवाला क्या करता है?

क्या तुमको मिठाई पसंद है?

III. सीखिये :

तुम हिन्दी सीखकर क्या करोगी?

मैं हिन्दी सीखकर भारत जाऊंगी।

मेरा भाई शाम को घर जाकर भोजन करेगा।

मेरी मां खाना बनाकर बच्चों को खिलाती है।

मेरे पिताजी खाना खाकर शहर जाते हैं।

वह अपना काम करके घर गया।

मेरे बड़े भाई कसरत करके लौटे।

Khaakar = having eaten

Karke = having done

My(n) Hindi seekhne ke baad Bharat ki yaatraa kar saktee hoo(n).

Khaanaa khaane ke baad turant sonaa tteek nahee(n) hai. (Turant = immediately)

Aap ghar pahu(n)chne ke baad mujhe chitthee likhiye.

Kaam pooraa karne ke baad chhuttee par jaana tteek hai.

Aap Delhi lautne ke baad phone keejiye.

Learn these forms:

Seekhne ke baad = after learning

Khaane ke baad = after eating

Pahu(n)chne ke baad = after reaching

Pooraa karne ke baad = after completing.

Lautne ke baad = after returning

IV. **Learn**

Number 81 - 100

81-90

Ikyaasee	Bayaasee	Tiraasee	Chauraasee	Pachaasee
Chhiyaasee	Satthaasee	Attaasee	Navaasee	Nabbe

91-100

Ikyaanave	Baanave	Tiraanave	Chauraanave	Panchaanave
Chhiyaanave	Satthaanave	Attaanave	Ninyaanave	Sau

Sau 100	Hazaar 1000	\Das hazaar 10,000
Lakh 100,000	Karoḍ = Crore/10 million	

मैं हिन्दी सीखने के बाद भारत की यात्रा कर सकती हूं।

खाना खाने के बाद तुरन्त सोना ठीक नहीं है।

आप घर पहुंचने के बाद मुझे चिट्ठी लिखिये।

काम पूरा करने के बाद छुट्टी पर जाना ठीक है।

आप दिल्ली लौटने के बाद फोन कीजिये।

IV. सीखिये :
संख्याएँ 81-100

81-90

इक्यासी	बयासी	तिरासी	चौरासी	पचासी
छियासी	सत्तासी	अड्ढासी	नवासी	नब्बे

91-100

इक्यानवे	बानवे	तिरानवे	चौरानवे	पंचानवे
छियानवे	सत्तानवे	अड्ढानवे	निन्यानवे	सौ

सौ 100	हज़ार 1000	दस हज़ार 10,000
लाख 100,000/lakh	करोड़ Crore/10 million	

Lesson - 9

I. Learn new words : (Naye shabd seekhiye)

Aaraam	comfort	Aaraam kar	to take rest
Bartaav/Vyavahaar	behaviour	Bartaav kar/Vyavahaar kar	to behave
Intazaam	arrangement	Intazaar	awaiting, expectation
Khabar*/Samaachaar	news	Akhbaar/Samaachaar patra	Newspaper
Lekh	essay	Lekhak	writer
Kavithaa	poetry	Kavayithree	poetess
Kavi	poet(m)	Naatak	play (stage play/drama)
Naatak'kaar	dramatist	Kahaanee*	story
Kahaaneekaar	story writer	Kalaa*	art
Kalaakaar	artist	Chitra/Tasveer*	picture
Chadh	to climb/ascend	Badh	to increase/grow
Utar	to descend/ge off	pighal	to melt
Badhaa	to increase/to extend (transitive)	Bhoo(n)k	to bark
Phisal	to slip	Garaj	to roar
Mimiyaa	to bleat (sheep)	Jal	to burn
Hinhinaa	to neigh	Bhar	to fill
Jalaa	to burn (Transitive)	Kharch kar	to spend
Kamaa	to earn	Ghir	to be surrounded
Gir	to fall		

II. Please answer (uttar deejiye) :

Aap kahaa(n) jaanaa chaahthe hai(n)?

Tum dookaan me(n) kyaa khareednaa chaahthe ho?

पाठ-9

I **नये शब्द सीखिये :**

आराम	आराम कर
बरताव / व्यवहार	बरताव कर / व्यवहार कर
इंतज़ाम	इन्तज़ार
खबर / समाचार	अखबार / समाचार पत्र
लेख	लेखक
कविता	कवयित्री
कवि	नाटक
नाटककार	कहानी
कहानीकार	कला
कलाकार	चित्र / तसवीर
चलचित्र	बढ़
चढ़	पिघल
उतर	भूंक
बढ़ा	गरज
फ़िसल	जल
मिमिया	भर
हिनहिना	खर्च कर
जला	घिर
कमा	
गिर	

II **उत्तर दीजिये :**

आप कहां जाना चाहते हैं?

तुम दूकान में क्या खरीदना चाहते हो?

Tumhaaraa dost ṣahar me(n) kyaa dekhnaa chaahthaa hai?

Aapke bhaayee kab gaa(n)v se aanaa chaahthe hai(n)?

Tumhaaree behan aaj kyaa karnaa chaahthee hai?

Bachche ṣaam ko kahaa(n) khelnaa chaahthe hai(n)?

Un bachcho(n) ko kyaa chaahiye?

Aapko aaj kahaa(n) jaanaa chaahiye?

Tumhaaree saheliyo(n) ko kitne phal chaahiye?

Bachcho(n) ko kitne baje school jaanaa chaahiye?

Tumko kyaa chaahiye?

Tumhaaree behan ko kyaa chaahiye?

Kyaa tum Hindi samajh saktee ho?

Kyaa aap ghoḍe par savaaree kar sakte hai(n)?

Kyaa ve laḍkiyaa(n) gaa saktee hai(n)?

Tum kitnee bhaashaaye(n) bol saktee ho?

Aapne aaj dopahar ko kyaa khaayaa?

Tumne aaj daftar me(n) kitne baje kaam shuroo kiyaa?
Aap daftar kitne baje gaye?

Aap daftar ke liye kitne baje nikle?

Aap apnee gaadee me(n) kahaa(n) jaaye(n) ge?

Vo bachchaa apnee maa(n) ke saath kahaa(n) jaa rahaa hai?

* III. Review   Uses of 'Chaahiye'*

A.   Bachcho(n) ko kyaa chaahiye?

Bachcho(n) ko khilaune chaahiye.

Tumhaare dost ko kyaa chaahiye?

Mere dost ko ek baḍaa ghar chaahiye.

Tumko kyaa chaahiye?

तुम्हारा दोस्त शहर में क्या देखना चाहता है?

आपके भाई कब गाँव से आना चाहते हैं?

तुम्हारी बहन आज क्या करना चाहती है?

बच्चे शाम को कहां खेलना चाहते हैं?

उन बच्चों को क्या चाहिए?

आपको आज कहां जाना चाहिए?

तुम्हारी सहेलियों को कितने फल चाहिए?

बच्चों को कितने बजे स्कूल जाना चाहिए?

तुमको क्या चाहिये?

तुम्हारी बहन को क्या चाहिए?

क्या तुम हिन्दी समझ सकती हो?

क्या आप घोड़े पर सवारी कर सकते हैं?

क्या वे लड़कियां गा सकती हैं?

तुम कितनी भाषाएँ बोल सकती हो?

आपने आज दोपहर को क्या खाया?

तुमने आज दफ़्तर में कितने बजे काम शुरू किया?

आप दफ़्तर कितने बजे गये?

आप दफ़्तर के लिए कितने बजे निकले?

आप अपनी गाड़ी में कहां जायेंगे?

वह बच्चा अपनी मां के साथ कहां जा रहा है?

III. Review

A. बच्चों को क्या चाहिये?

बच्चों को खिलौने चाहिये?

तुम्हारे दोस्त को क्या चाहिये?

मेरे दोस्त को एक बड़ा घर चाहिये।

तुमको क्या चाहिये?

Mujhe ek nayee motor gaaḍee chaahiye.

B. Bachcho! tum logo(n) ko jaldee ghar pahu(n)chanaa chaahiye.

Aapko hameṣaa Hindi me(n) bolnaa chaahiye.

Bharat me(n) sabko Hindi seekhnee chaahiye.

Tumko samay par daftar pahu(n)chnaa chaahiye.

Learn the following :

Use of 'Pasand'*

C. Mujhe aam pasand hai.

Bachcho(n) ko mittayee pasand hai.

Kyaa aapko New York pasand hai?

Jee haa(n), lekin mujhe Chicago zyaada pasand hai.

Use of 'Maaloom'*

D. Kyaa tumko Hindi maaloom hai?

Jee haa(n), mujhe Hindi maaloom hai.

Mujhe aapke ghar kaa pathaa maaloom hai. (pathaa = address)

Mere dost ko Hindi ke alaavaa aur teen-chaar bhaashaaye(n) maaloom hai(n).

Note :

aur = and, 'aur' also means 'other' and 'more'

Chaahiye = need; also used as an auxiliary verb to denote 'must/should/ought to'.

Also see foot notes on pages 84 and 85.

Pasand = like Maaloom = know

When the above are used in sentences as main or auxiliary verbs, the preposition 'Ko' (postposition) should be added to the subject.

मुझे एक नयी मोटर गाड़ी चाहिये।

B. बच्चो! तुम लोगों को जल्दी घर पहुंचना चाहिये।
आपको हमेशा हिन्दी में बोलना चाहिये।
भारत में सबको हिन्दी सीखनी चाहिये।
तुमको समय पर दफ़्तर पहुंचना चाहिये।

सीखिये :

C. मुझे आम पसन्द है।
बच्चों को मिठाई पसन्द है।
क्या आपको न्यूयार्क पसन्द है।
जी हां, लेकिन मुझे शिकागो ज़्यादा पसन्द है।

D. क्या तुमको हिन्दी मालूम है?
जी हां, मुझे हिन्दी मालूम है।
मुझे आपके घर का पता मालूम है।
मेरे दोस्त को हिन्दी के अलावा और तीन-चार भाषाएँ मालूम हैं।

Lesson - 10

I. Naye Shabd (New Words) :

Chaaval	rice	Dhaan	paddy
Gehoo(n)	wheat	Makayee	maize
Daal	lentil	Toor	red gram
Uḍad	black gram	Matar	peas
Masoor	a variety of red gram	Besan	bengal gram
Kaaju	cashew nut	Baadaam	almond
Jahaaz	ship	Havaayee Jahaaz	aeroplane
Pandubbee	submarine	Naav*/Naukaa*	boat
Naukaa-ghar	house boat		

Vaapas aa	return/come back	Vaapas jaa	return/go back
Laut	return (for coming back/ going back)		
Chhoo	touch	Dhokhaa khaa	to be cheated
Dhokhaa de	to cheat	Havaa khaa	to take a stroll
De de	to give away	le le	to take away
Chalaa jaa	to go away	Bytt jaa	to sit (to say by force)
Kar le	to do (for self)	Kar de	to do (emphasis)
Dekh le	to see (for self)	Paḍh le	to read (for self)

II. Please answer :

Aap baazaar me(n) kyaa khareede(n)ge?

Aajkal dookaan me(n) kaun-se achchhe phal milthe hai(n)?

Ye(h) nayee kithaab kahaa(n) milthee hai?

Aap us dost se kab aur kahaa(n) mile?

पाठ-10

I नये शब्द :

चावल	धान
गेहूं	मकई
दाल	तूर
उड़द	मटर
मसूर	बेसन
काजू	बादाम
जहाज़	हवाई जहाज़
पनडुब्बी	नाव/नौका
नौका-घर	

वापस आ	वापस जा
लौट	
छू	धोखा खा
धोखा दे	हवा खा
दे दे	ले ले
चला जा	बैठ जा
कर ले	कर दे
देख ले	पढ़ ले

II उत्तर दीजिये :

आप बाज़ार में क्या खरीदेंगे?

आजकल दूकान में कौन-से अच्छे फल मिलते हैं?

यह नई किताब कहां मिलती है?

आप उस दोस्त से कब और कहां मिले?

Kyaa tum ṣahar me(n) apne bhaayee se milogee?

Tumne ye(h) kahaanee kab likhee?

Tum aaj sabere kahaa(n) gaye?

Tumhaare rishtedaar havaayee adde se kitne baje ghar aaye?

Aapne kab Hindi seekhee?

Aapne aaj kitne ghante kaam kiyaa?

Kyaa tum vahaa(n) Hindi me(n) bole?

Tumhaare bhaayee dookaan se kyaa laaye?

Aapko kitne baje daftar jaanaa chaahiye?

Bachche aaj sabere se kahaa(n) gaye hai(n)?

Kyaa unke pitaajee bhee unke saath gaye hai(n)?

Kyaa ve log akele ṣahar jaa sakthe hai(n)?

Pichhle saal aap kahaa(n) gaye the?

Kyaa aapkee behno(n) ne dookaan me(n) aam khareedaa thaa?

Kyaa tumne bhee kuchh khareedaa hai?

Kyaa aapke bachche tasveer banaa sakthe hai(n)?

III. Fill in the blanks:

My(n) ṣahar se kal ....

Tum kitne baje daftar ....?

Mujhe aam ....

Bachche school se lautne .... thoḍee der ....

Aaj havaayee jahaaz der se ....

Meree sahelee ko achchhe-achchhe kapḍe ....

Aapko hamaare ghar zaroor ....

Bharat ke .... me(n) Himalay hai.

Sardee ke mausam me(n) garam kapḍe ....

My(n) ghar se .... nikalthaa hoo(n) aur .... daftar pahu(n)chthaa hoo(n)

Meree behan .... coffee peethee hai.

क्या तुम शहर में अपने भाई से मिलोगी?

तुमने यह कहानी कब लिखी?

तुम आज सबेरे कहां गये?

तुम्हारे रिश्तेदार हवाई अड्डे से कितने बजे घर आये?

आपने कब हिन्दी सीखी?

आपने आज कितने घंटे काम किया?

क्या तुम वहां हिन्दी में बोले?

तुम्हारे भाई दूकान से क्या लाये?

आपको कितने बजे दफ़्तर जाना चाहिए?

बच्चे आज सबेरे से कहां गये हैं?

क्या उनके पिताजी भी उनके साथ गये हैं?

क्या वे लोग अकेले शहर जा सकते हैं?

पिछले साल आप कहां गये थे?

क्या आपकी बहनों ने दूकान में आम खरीदा था?

क्या तुमने भी कुछ खरीदा है?

क्या आपके बच्चे तसवीर बना सकते हैं?

III. **खाली जगहें भरिये :**

मैं शहर से कल ....

तुम कितने बजे दफ़्तर ....

मुझे आम ....

बच्चे स्कूल से लौटने .... थोड़ी देर ....

आज हवाई जहाज देर से ....

मेरी सहेली को अच्छे-अच्छे कपड़े ....

आपको हमारे घर ज़रूर ....

भारत के .... में हिमालय है।

सरदी के मौसम में गरम कपड़े ....

मैं घर से .... निकलता हूं और .... दफ़्तर पहुंचता हूं।

मेरी बहन .... काफी पीती है।

Bachche school .... kyaa karthe hai(n)?

Tum Hindi .... kyaa karogee?

Humne dookaan me(n) mittaaiyaa(n) ....

Humaare ghar .... yek bageechaa hai.

My(n) bhaayee ke liye ṣahar se ....

Rail Gaaḍee .... Station ....?

Meree behan khoob Hindi ....

My(n) aaj darje ke baad jaldee ghar ....

*IV. Paḍhiye aur Samjhiye :

A. Hindi kakshaa kal se shuroo ho rahee hai.

Kakshaa saaḍhe paa(n)ch baje se hogee.

Aap aur aapki behene(n) kakshaa me(n) zaroor aa sakthee hai(n).

Mere bhaayee Hindi seekhnaa chaahthe hai(n). **Kyaa ve bhee kakshaa me(n) aa sakthe hai(n).**

Aapke bhaaiyo(n) ko pahlee kakshaa me(n) aanaa chaahiye. Kal kee kakshaa doosre **sthar** kee hai. **sthar = standard/level**

Aap kal zaroor kakshaa men(n) aaiye.

Pahlee kakshaa parso(n) hogee; aapke bhaayee usme(n) aaye(n)ge.

Hum kal kakshaa me(n) mile(n)ge. Kakshaa* (darjaa) = class   Sthar = standard, level

B. Meraa dost ek saal pahle Hindi seekhne lagaa.

Mere dost kee baḍee behan school me(n) Hindi sikhaane lagee.

Hum log apne maa(n)-baap ke saath mandir jaane lage.

Meree betiyaa(n) sangeet seekhne lagee(n).

Kyaa aapkaa bhaayee gaa saktaa hai?

Nahee(n), vo pichhle saal hee gaanaa seekhne lagaa. Shaayad agle saal yaa do-teen saal ke baad vo gaa sakegaa.

Bachchaa nau baje sone lagaa.

Bachche nau baje sone lage.

बच्चे स्कूल .... क्या करते हैं।

तुम हिन्दी .... क्या करोगी?

हमने दूकान में मिठाइयां ....

हमारे घर .... एक बगीचा है।

मैं भाई के लिए शहर से ....

रेलगाड़ी .... स्टेशन ....?

मेरी बहन खूब हिन्दी ....

मैं आज दर्जे के बाद जल्दी घर ....

IV. पढ़िये और समझिये :

अ. हिन्दी कक्षा कल से शुरू हो रही है।

कक्षा साढ़े पांच बजे से होगी।

आप और आपकी बहनें कक्षा में ज़रूर आ सकती हैं।

मेरे भाई हिन्दी सीखना चाहते हैं। क्या वे भी कक्षा में आ सकते हैं?

आपके भाइयों को पहली कक्षा में आना चाहिये। कल की कक्षा दूसरे स्तर की है।

आप कल जरूर कक्षा में आइये।

पहली कक्षा परसों होगी, आपके भाई उसमें आयेंगे।

हम कल कक्षा में मिलेंगे।

आ. मेरा दोस्त एक साल पहले हिन्दी सीखने लगा।

मेरे दोस्त की बड़ी बहन स्कूल में हिन्दी सिखाने लगी।

हम लोग अपने मां-बाप के साथ मंदिर जाने लगे।

मेरी बेटियां संगीत सीखने लगीं।

क्या आपका भाई गा सकता है?

नहीं, वह पिछले साल ही गाना सीखने लगा। शायद अगले साल या दो-तीन साल के बाद वह गा सकेगा।

बच्चा नौ बजे सोने लगा।

बच्चे नौ बजे सोने लगे।

Bachchee nau baje sone lagee.

Bachchiyaa(n) nau baje sone lagee(n).

! ve! log cinema dekhkar Hindi me(n) bolne lagthe hai(n).

Meraa betaa bhee thoḍaa-thoḍaa bolne lagthaa hai.

Kyaa aap bhee Hindi me(n) bolne lage(n)ge?

Jee haa(n), par is saal nahee(n); agle saal my(n) Hindi me(n) bolne lagoo(n)gaa.

Sangeet = music Ṣhaayad = perhaps par = on; but

C. Mere pitajee beemaar the; isliye mujhe kal gaa(n)v jaanaa paḍaa.

Humko chaaval bahut pasand hai. Lekin restoraan me(n) chaaval nahee(n) thaa; Isliye humko rotee khaanee paḍee.

Sabko roz aatt ghante kaam karana paḍthaa hai.

Mujhe kal se roz havaayee addaa jaanaa paḍegaa; kyonki my(n) kal se vahaa(n) kaam karne lagoongaa.

Vahaa(n) mujhe Punjabi me(n) bolnaa paḍegaa. Hume(n) bhee kabhee kabhee panjabi me(n) bolna paḍthaa hai.

Meree behan bhee Punjabi seekhne lagee.

Restaurant = Restoraan

D. Hum log pahle Uttar Pradesh me(n) rahthe the.

Isliye hum sab khoob Hindi bolthe the.

Meree betee bhee Hindi bolthee thee.

Lekin meree behne(n) Hindi nahee(n) bolthee thee(n). Isliye ve pichhle saal Hindi seekhne lagee(n).

Ye(h) Ashok hai. Ye(h) mere dost ka betaa hai.

Ashok pahle roz humaare ghar aathaa thaa.

Ashok kee maa(n) college me(n) paḍhaathee thee(n).

Meraa dost railway me(n) kaam karthaa thaa.

Ashok aur uske maa(n)-baap agle maheene Dillee jaaye(n)ge.

Hum log chuttiyo(n) me(n) unse mile(n)ge.   **Dillee = Delhi**

बच्ची नौ बजे सोने लगी।

बच्चियां नौ बजे सोने लगीं।

वे लोग सिनेमा देखकर हिन्दी में बोलने लगते हैं।

मेरा बेटा भी थोड़ा-थोड़ा बोलने लगता है।

क्या आप भी हिन्दी में बोलने लगेंगे?

जी हां, पर इस साल नहीं, अगले साल मैं हिन्दी में बोलने लगूंगा।

इ. मेरे पिताजी बीमार थे; इसलिए मुझे कल गांव जाना पड़ा।

हमको चावल बहुत पसन्द है। लेकिन रेस्तोरां में चावल नहीं था। इसलिए हमको रोटी खानी पड़ी।

सबको रोज आठ घंटे काम करना पड़ता है।

मुझे कल से रोज हवाई अड्डा जाना पड़ेगा; क्योंकि मैं कल से वहां काम करने लगूंगा।

वहां मुझे पंजाबी में बोलना पड़ेगा।

हमें भी कभी-कभी पंजाबी में बोलना पड़ता है।

मेरी बहन भी पंजाबी सीखने लगी।

ई. हम लोग पहले उत्तर प्रदेश में रहते थे।

इसलिए हम सब खूब हिन्दी बोलते थे।

मेरी बेटी भी हिन्दी बोलती थी।

लेकिन मेरी बहनें हिन्दी नहीं बोलती थीं। इसलिए वे पिछले साल हिन्दी सीखने लगीं।

यह अशोक है। यह मेरे दोस्त का बेटा है।

अशोक पहले रोज़ हमारे घर आता था।

अशोक की मां कालेज में पढ़ाती थीं।

मेरा दोस्त रेलवे में काम करता था।

अशोक और उसके मां-बाप अगले महीने दिल्ली जायेंगे।

हम लोग छुट्टियों में उनसे मिलेंगे।

Naye Shabd (New Words) : Metals, Minerals, etc.

Peethal = brass	Koylaa = coal	Thaambaa = copper	Sonaa = gold
Lohaa = iron	Chaa(n)dee = silver	Heeraa = diamond	Pannaa = emerald
Seesaa = lead	Chumbak = magnet	Paaraa = mercury	Mothee = pearl
Faulaad = steel	Gandhak = sulphur	Jasthaa = zink	Abhrak = mica

Names of diseases

Beemaaree = disease

Damaa = asthma	Haijaa = cholera	Jukaam (Sardee) = cold
Kabz = constipation	Khaa(n)see = cough	Bukhaar = fever	Sir-Dard = headache
Dard = pain	Apach (Badhajmee) = indigestion	
Pechish = dysentery	Sir Chakraanaa = dizziness	Lakvaa = paralysis
Behoṣee (Moorchaa) = fainting	Phunsee = pimple	Chechak = smallpox
Soojan = swelling	Ghaav (Zakhm) = wound	

Dhanyavaad/shukriyaa = Thanks

Rules:

* The Students should be introduced to the following forms. These can be reviewed while beginning the Advanced Course.

1. Use of LAG

'Lag' indicates beginning of an action; but it is used as an auxiliary verb with the modified infinitive form of a main verb. The main verb will remain with the suffix 'ne', i.e. karne, jaane, aane, seekhne, etc. but 'lag' will change according to the tense, gender and number of the subject :

a. Bachchaa bolne lagthaa hai. The child begins to speak.
Bachche khelne lagthe hai(n). Children begin to play.
Bachchee bolne lagthee hai. The girl begins to speak.
Bachchiyaa(n) khelne lagthee hai(n). Girls begin to play.

b. Meraa bhaayee Hindi seekhne lagaa. My brother began to learn Hindi.
Mere pitaajee daftar jaane lage. My father began to go to office.
Meree behan school jaane lagee. My sister began to go to school.
Meree behne(n) Hindi bolne lagee(n). My sisters began to speak Hindi.

V. नये शब्द धातु, खनिज पदार्थ, वगैरह   Precious Stones)

पीतल	कोयला	तांबा	सोना
लोहा	चांदी	हीरा	पन्ना
सीसा	चुम्बक	पारा	मोती
फ़ौलाद	गन्धक	जस्ता	अभ्रक

Names of disease

दमा	हैजा	जुकाम (सर्दी)	कब्ज
खांसी	बुखार	सिर-दर्द	दर्द
अपच (बदहजमी)	**बीमारी**	पेचिश	सिर चकराना
लकवा	बेहाशी (मूर्छा)	फुंसी	चेचक
सूजन	घाव (जख्म)		

धन्यवाद / शुक्रिया

---

c.   My(n) kal se kasrat karne lagoo(n)gaa. I will begin to do exercise from tomorrow.

Kyaa aap bhee kasrat karne lage(n)ge? Will you also begin to do exercise?

Meree betee kaam karne lagegee. My daughter will begin to work.

Meree behne(n) chaar baje khelne lage(n)gee. My sisters will begin to play at 4 o'clock.

2.   **Use of 'PAD'**

'Pad' is an auxiliary verb and will be used with the infinitive from of a main verb. 'Pad' is used to express force or complusion. The subject will stand in the dative case. The verbs–both main and auxiliary–will agree with the object in gender and number.

Raam ko van jaanaa paḍaa. Rama had to go to forest.

Bachcho(n) ko sabere school jaanaa paḍaa. Children had to go to school in the morning.

Peter ko tasveer banaanee paḍee. Peter had to draw a picture.

Mere dosto(n) ko college me(n) kayee bhaashaaye(n) seekhnee paḍee(n). My friends had to learn many languages in the college.

'Paḍ' can also be used in present and future tenses.

3.   The following forms are in past tense and indicate habit; we may call these forms as 'habitual past'.

Karthaa thaa; Karthe the; Karthee thee, Karthee thee(n) - used to do.

Bolthaa thaa; Bolthe the; Bolthee thee; Bolthee thee(n). - used to speak.

Seekhthaa thaa; Seekhthe the; Seekhthee thee; Seekhthee thee(n) - used to learn

Appendix

Chart (Saaraṇee)

BYTT = sit

Masculine	Feminine
I. My(n) bytt thaa hoo(n)	My(n) bytt thee hoo(n)
Tum bytt the ho	Tum bytt thee ho
Vo/ye(h) bytt thaa hai	Vo/ye(h) bytt thee hai

Hum ⎤	Hum ⎤
Aap ⎬ bytt the hai(n)	Aap ⎬ bytt thee hai(n)
Ve/Ye ⎦	Ve/Ye ⎦

II. My(n) bytt rahaa hoo(n)	My(n) bytt rahee hoo(n)
Tum bytt rahe ho	Tum bytt rahee ho
Vo/ye(h) bytt rahaa hai	Vo/ye(h) bytt rahee hai

Hum ⎤	Hum ⎤
Aap ⎬ bytt rahe hai(n)	Aap ⎬ bytt rahee hai(n)
Ve/Ye ⎦	Ve/ye ⎦

III. My(n) bytt rahaa thaa	My(n) bytt rahee thee
Tum bytt rahe the	Tum bytt rahee thee(n)
Vo/ye(h) bytt rahaa tha	Vo/ye(h) bytt rahee thee

Hum ⎤	Hum ⎤
Aap ⎬ bytt rahe the	Aap ⎬ bytt rahee thee(n)
Ve/Ye ⎦	Ve/Ye ⎦

IV. My(n) byttoo(n)gaa	My(n) byttoo(n)gee
Tum byttoge	Tum byttogee

परिशिष्ट

चार्ट (सारणी)

बैठ

Masculine	Feminine

I मैं बैठता हूं   मैं बैठती हूं
तुम बैठते हो   तुम बैठती हो
वह/यह बैठता है   वह/यह बैठती है

हम ⌐   हम ⌐
आप ⊢ बैठते हैं   आप ⊢ बैठती हैं
वे/ये ⌐   वे/ये ⌐

II मैं बैठ रहा हूं   मैं बैठ रही हूं
तुम बैठ रहे हो   तुम बैठ रही हो
वह/यह बैठ रहा है   वह/यह बैठ रही है

हम ⌐   हम ⌐
आप ⊢ बैठ रहे हैं   आप ⊢ बैठ रही हैं
वे/ये ⌐   वे/ये ⌐

III मैं बैठ रहा था   मैं बैठ रही थी
तुम बैठ रहे थे   तुम बैठ रही थीं
वह/यह बैठ रहा था   वह/यह बैठ रही थी

हम ⌐   हम ⌐
आप ⊢ बैठ रहे थे   आप ⊢ बैठ रही थीं
वे/ये ⌐   वे/ये ⌐

IV मैं बैठूंगा   मैं बैठूंगी
तुम बैठोगे   तुम बैठोगी

Vo/ye(h) byttege

Hum ─┐
Aap ─├─bytte(n)ge
Ve/Ye ─┘

Vo/ye(h) byettegee

Hum ─┐
Aap ─├─bytte(n)gee
Ve/Ye ─┘

V. My(n) byttaa
Tum bytte
Vo/ye(h) byttaa
Hum/Aap/Ve/Ye bytte

My(n) byttee
Tum byttee(n)
Vo/ye(h) byttee
Hum/Aap/Ve/Ye byttee(n)

VI. My(n) byttaa hoo(n)
Tum bytte ho
Vo/ye(h) byttaa hai
Hum/Aap/Ve/Ye bytte hai(n)

My(n) bytee hoo(n)
Tum byttee ho
Vo/ye(h) byttee hai
Hum/Aap/Ve/Ye byttee hai(n)

VII. My(n) byttaa thaa
Tum bytte the
Vo/ye(h) byttaa thaa
Hum/Aap/Ve/Ye byte the

My(n) byttee thee
Tum byttee thee(n)
Vo/ye(h) bytee thee
Hum/Aap/Ve/Ye byttee thee(n)

KHAA = eat

Masculine

Feminine

I. My(n) mittaayee khaathaa hoo(n)
My(n) mittaayee khaa rahaa hoo(n)
My(n) mittaayee khaa rahaa thaa
My(n) mittaayee khaaoo(n)gaa
My(n) ne mittaayee khaayee
My(n) ne mittaayee khaayee hai
My(n) ne mittaayee khaayee thee

khaathee hoo(n)
khaa rahee hoo(n)
khaa rahee thee
khaaoo(n)gee
khaayee
khaayee hai
khaayee thee

वह/यह बैठेगा   वह/यह बैठेगी

हम ⌐   हम ⌐
आप ├ बैठेंगे   आप ├ बैठेंगी
वे/ये ⌐   वे/ये ⌐

V मैं बैठा   मैं बैठी
   तुम बैठे   तुम बैठीं
   वह/यह बैठा   वह/यह बैठी

   हम ⌐   हम ⌐
   आप ├ बैठे   आप ├ बैठीं
   वे/ये ⌐   वे/ये ⌐

VI मैं बैठा हूं   मैं बैठी हूं
    तुम बैठे हो   तुम बैठी हो
    वह/यह बैठा है   वह/यह बैठी है
    हम/आप/वे/ये बैठे हैं   हम/आप/वे/ये बैठी हैं

VII मैं बैठा था   मैं बैठी थी
    तुम बैठे थे   तुम बैठी थीं
    वह/यह बैठा था   वह/यह बैठी थी
    हम/आप/वे/ये बैठे थे   हम/आप/वे/ये बैठी थीं

खा

Masculine	Feminine
I मैं मिठाई खाता हूं	खाती हूं
मैं मिठाई खा रहा हूं	खा रही हूं
मैं मिठाई खा रहा था	खा रही थी
मैं मिठाई खाऊंगा	खाऊंगी
मैंने मिठाई खायी	खायी
मैंने मिठाई खायी है	खायी है
मैंने मिठाई खायी थी	खायी थी

II. Tum mittaayee khaathe ho   khaathee ho

Tum mittaayee khaa rahe ho   khaa rahee ho

Tum mittaayee khaa rahe the   khaa rahee thee(n)

Tum mittaayee khaaoge   khaaogee

Tumne mittaayee khaayee   khaayee

Tumne mittaayee khaayee hai   khaayee hai

Tumne mittaayee khaayee thee   khaayee thee

III. Vo/ye(h) mittaayee khaathaa hai   khaathee hai

Vo/ye(h) mittaayee khaa rahaa hai   khaa rahee hai

Vo/ye(h) mittaayee khaa rahaa thaa   khaa rahee thee

Vo/ye(h) mittaayee khaayegaa   khaayegee

Usne/Isne mittaayee khaayee   khaayee

Usne/Isne mittaayee khaayee hai   khaayee hai

Usne/Isne mittaayee khaayee thee   Khaayee thee

VI. Hum/Aap/Ve/Ye mittaayee khaathe hai(n)   khaathee hai(n)

Hum/Aap/Ve/Ye mittaayee khaa rahe hai(n)   khaa rahee hai(n)

Hum/Aap/Ve/Ye mittaayee khaa rahe the   khaa rahee thee(n)

Hum/Aap/Ve/Ye mittaayee khaaye(n)ge   khaaye(n)gee

Humne)   ⌐ mittaayee khaayee   khaayee

Apne)   ├─ mittaayee khaayee hai   khaayee hai

Unho(n)ne/Inho(n)ne⌐   mittaayee khaayee thee   khaayee thee

II तुम मिठाई खाते हो   खाती हो

    तुम मिठाई खा रहे हो   खा रही हो

    तुम मिठाई खा रहे थे   खा रही थीं

    तुम मिठाई खाओगे   खाओगी

    तुमने मिठाई खायी   खायी

    तुमने मिठाई खायी है   खायी है

    तुमने मिठाई खायी थी   खायी थी

III वह/यह मिठाई खाता है   खाती है

    वह/यह मिठाई खा रहा है   खा रही है

    वह/यह मिठाई खा रहा था   खा रही थी

    वह/यह मिठाई खायेगा   खायेगी

    उसने/इसने मिठाई खायी   खायी

    उसने/इसने मिठाई खायी है   खायी है

    उसने/इसने मिठाई खायी थी   खायी थी

IV हम/आप/वे/ये   मिठाई खाते हैं   खाती हैं

    हम/आप/वे/ये   मिठाई खा रहे हैं   खा रही हैं

    हम/आप/वे/ये   मिठाई खा रहे थे   खा रही थीं

    हम/आप/वे/ये   मिठाई खायेंगे   खायेंगी

    हमने/आपने/उन्होंने/इन्होंने   मिठाई खायी   खायी

                               मिठाई खायी है   खायी है

                               मिठाई खायी थी   खायी थी

Part III

Hindi Course (Advanced)

Session III

10 Lessons

Session III (Advanced)

Lesson - 1

I. Paḍhiye:

Aaiye; Consulate me(n) aapka swaagat hai.

Aaj hum Hindi ki nayee kakshaa shuroo kar rahe hai(n).

Ye(h) nayee kakshaa teen maheene ke baad shuroo ho rahee hai.

Kyo(n)ki pichhlee kakshaa December maheene me(n) khatam huee thee.

Aap log roz Hindi ke liye thoḍaa samay nikaaliye.

Koyee bhee bhaashaa seekhne ke liye aadat aur dhyaan kee zoroorat hai.

Kakshaa me(n) savaa yaa deḍh ghanta paḍhte hai(n)/seekhthe hai(n).

Phir ek hafte ke baad hum milenge.

Isliye beech me(n) roz pandrah-bees minute kaa samay nikaalkar Hindi paḍhne aur bolne kee koshish keejiye.

Aap log das kakshaao(n) ke baad Hindi me(n) bol sake(n)ge.

Aaiye; Hum aaj barsaat ke baare me(n) ek paatt paḍhe(n).

II. Barsaat

Garmee ke baad barsaat aathee hai.

Barsaat kaa mausam bahut zarooree hai.

Barsaat kee pehlee bauchhaar bahut achchhee lagthee hai.

Garmee ke baad is mausam me(n) log chain kee saa(n)s lethe hai(n).

Kuch desho(n) me(n) barsaat ke mausam me(n) beemaariyaa(n) phailthee hai(n).

Kyo(n)ki vahaa(n) makkhee-machchaḍ aur keeḍe-makauḍe bahut zyaada takleef dethe hai(n).

Achchhee sabziyaa(n) bhee nahee(n) milthee hai(n).

Saḍko(n) par paanee bhar jaathaa hai.

Par, America me(n) achchhee suvidhaaye(n) hai(n).

तीसरा सत्र (उच्च स्तर)

पाठ – 1

I. पढ़िये :

आइये, कान्सुलेट में आपका स्वागत है।

आज हम हिन्दी की नयी कक्षा शुरू कर रहे हैं।

यह नयी कक्षा तीन महीने के बाद शुरू हो रही है।

क्योंकि पिछली कक्षा दिसम्बर महीने में खतम हुई थी।

आप लोग रोज़ हिन्दी के लिए थोड़ा समय निकालिये।

कोई भी भाषा सीखने के लिए आदत और ध्यान की ज़रूरत है।

कक्षा में सवा या डेढ़ घंटा पढ़ते हैं/सीखते हैं।

फिर एक हफ़्ते के बाद हम मिलेंगे।

इसलिये बीच में रोज़ पन्द्रह-बीस मिनट का समय निकालकर हिन्दी पढ़ने और बोलने की कोशिश कीजिये।

आप लोग दस कक्षाओं के बाद हिन्दी में बोल सकेंगे।

आइये; हम आज बरसात के बारे में एक पाठ पढ़ें।

II. बरसात

गरमी के बाद बरसात आती है।

बरसात का मौसम बहुत ज़रूरी है।

बरसात की पहली बौछार बहुत अच्छी लगती है।

गरमी के बाद इस मौसम में लोग चैन की सांस लेते हैं।

कुछ देशों में बरसात के मौसम में बीमारियां फैलती हैं।

क्योंकि वहां मक्खी-मच्छड़ और कीड़े-मकौड़े बहुत ज़्यादा तकलीफ़ देते हैं।

अच्छी सब्जियां भी नहीं मिलती हैं।

सड़कों पर पानी भर जाता है।

पर, अमेरिका में अच्छी सुविधाएँ हैं।

Yahaa(n) chhote-baḍe sabko barsaat achchhee lagthee hai.

Barsaat ke mausam me(n) insaano(n) ke alaavaa peḍ-paudhe bhee khush hothe hai(n).

Ab aap bathaaiye, aapko barsaat kaa mausam kysaa lagthaa hai?

Aapko kysaa lagtaa hai? How do you like?

Insaan = human being

Makkhee* = fly

Keeḍe-Makauḍe = insects

Beemaaree* = sickness

Chain kee saa(n)s* le = to have a sigh of relief

Chain = ease of mind; contentment/relief

Saa(n)s* = Breath

Zarooree = necessary/essential

Suvidhaa* = facility

Machchaḍ/Machchar = mosquito

Bahut Zyaada = too many/too much

Bathaa = to tell / describe/ show

Bauchhaar* = shower

Bhar = fill

Bhar jaata hai = gets filled   Aadat* = habit   Dhar jaata hai = gets filled

Shuroo ho x khatam ho ⎤

Shuroo kar x khatam kar ⎦ — Learn the difference

यहां छोटे-बड़े सबको बरसात अच्छी लगती है।

बरसात के मौसम में इनसानों के अलावा पेड़-पौधे भी खुश होते हैं।

अब आप बताइये, आपको बरसात का मौसम कैसा लगता है?

आपको कैसा लगता है?	How do you like?

इनसान = human being   सुविधा = facility   मक्खी = fly

मच्छड़/मच्छर = mosquito   कीड़े-मकौड़े = insects   बहुत ज़्यादा = too many/too much

बीमारी = sickness   बता = to tell/describe/show

चैन की सांस ले = to have a sigh of relief   चैन = ease of mind, contentment, relief

सांस = breath   बौछार = shower   ज़रूरी = necessary/essential

भर = fill   भर जाता है = gets filled

आदत = habit   ध्यान = concentration

शुरू हो × खतम हो ⎤— Learn the difference
शुरू कर × खतम कर ⎦

Lesson - 2

I. Paḍhiye :   BHAARAT

Bhaarat bahut baḍaa desh hai.   Ye(h) bahut puraanaa desh hai.

Iske uttar me(n) Himaalay Pahaaḍ hai. Dakshin me(n) Hind Mahaasaagar hai.

Poorv me(n) Bengal kee khaaḍee hai.   Paschim me(n) Arab Saagar hai.

Bhaarat me(n) kayee baḍee nadiyaa(n) hai(n).

Gangaa sabse baḍee aur pavitra nadee hai.

Bhaarat kee rajdhaanee Nayee Dillee hai.

Dillee sundar ṣahar hai.

Mumbai, Kolkata aur Chennai bhee baḍe ṣahar hai(n).

Bhaarat kee aabaadi bahut zyaadaa hai.

Ab vo ek arab se aage pahu(n)ch gayee hai.

Desh = country	Puraanaa = old	Nayaa = new
Uttar = north	Dakshin = south	Poorva, Poorab = east
Paschim = west	Pahaaḍ = mountain	Hind Mahaasaagar = Indian Ocean
Bangal kee khaaḍee = Bay of Bengal		Arab Saagar = Arabian Sea
Nadee* = river	Sabse Baḍee = biggest	Pavitra = holy
Rajdhaanee* = capital	Aabaadee* = population	Arab = 1000 million
Se Aage = beyond	Pahu(n)ch Gayee Hai = has reached	

पाठ - 2

I. पढ़िये :

भारत

भारत बहुत बड़ा देश है।

इसके उत्तर में हिमालय पहाड़ है।

पूर्व में बंगाल की खाड़ी है।

भारत में कई बड़ी नदियां हैं।

गंगा सबसे बड़ी और पवित्र नदी है।

भारत की राजधानी नई दिल्ली है।

दिल्ली सुन्दर शहर है।

मुम्बई, कोलकाता और चेन्नै भी बड़े शहर हैं।

भारत की आबादी बहुत ज़्यादा है।

अब वह एक अरब से आगे पहुंच गयी है।

यह बहुत पुराना देश है।

दक्षिण में हिन्द महासागर है।

पश्चिम में अरब सागर है।

देश = country

उत्तर = north

पश्चिम = west

बंगाल की खाड़ी = Bay of Bengal

नदी = river

राजधानी = capital

से आगे = beyond

पुराना = old

दक्षिण = south

पहाड़ = mountain

सबसे बड़ी = biggest

आबादी = population

पहुंच गयी है = has reached

नया = new

पूर्व, पूरब = east

हिन्द महासागर = Indian Ocean

अरब सागर = Arabian Sea

पवित्र = holy

अरब = 1000 million

II. Baathcheeth* (discussion / dialogue) :

Kyaa aap Anita aur uske bhaayee Ram ko jaanthe hai(n)?

Jee nahee(n), my(n) nahee(n) jaanthaa.

Ve aapke paḍos me(n) rahthe hai(n).

Mujhe afsos hai ki my(n) unse kabhee nahee(n) milaa hoo(n).

Aap unse zaroor miliye; ve mere achchhe dost hai(n).

Zaroor miloo(n)gaa.

Ram bahut dilchasp aadmee hai. Anita bhee bahut achchhee hai.

My(n) unko pichhle pandrah saalo(n) se jaanthaa hoo(n).

Kyaa aap log saath-saath paḍhthe the?

Jee haa(n), hum log yek hee college me(n) paḍhthe the.

Bahut achchhee baat hai. My(n) bahut jaldee unse milne kee koshish karoo(n)gaa.

Aap mujhe unkaa sahee pataa deejiye. Unkaa telephone number bhee deejiye.

My(n) pahle unko telephone karoo(n)gaa. Phir unse miloo(n)gaa.

Achchha, leejiye unkaa pataa aur telephone number. Aap unse zaroor miliye.

Paḍos me(n) = in the neighborhood	Paḍosee = neighbor
Afsos, Dukh = regret (sadness)	Dilchasp = interesting
Dilchaspee = interest	Sahee = correct
Pataa = address	Zaroor, Avashya = surely

III. Numbers 1-50 (Review) :

1-10	Ek	Do	Teen	Chaar	Paa(n)ch
	Chhe	Saath	Aatt	Nau	Das
11-20	Gyaarah	Baarah	Terah	Chaudah	Pandrah
	Solah	Satrah	Attaarah	Unnees	Bees
21-30	Ikkees	Baayees	Teyees	Chaubees	Pachchees
	Chabbees	Sattaayees	Attaayees	Untees	Tees
31-40	Ikthees	Baththees	Tai(n)thees	Chau(n)thees	Py(n)thees
	Chaththees	Sai(n)thees	Aḍthees	Unthaaless	Chaalees
41-50	Ikthaalees	Bayaalees	Tai(n)thaalees	Chavaalees	Py(n)thaalees
	Chhiyaalees	Sai(n)thaalees	Aḍthaalees	Unchaas	Pachaas

II. बातचीत :

क्या आप अनीता और उसके भाई राम को जानते हैं?

जी नहीं, मैं नहीं जानता।

वे आपके पड़ोस में रहते हैं।

मुझे अफ़सोस है कि मैं उनसे कभी नहीं मिला हूं।

आप उनसे ज़रूर मिलिये, वे मेरे अच्छे दोस्त हैं।

ज़रूर मिलूंगा।

राम बहुत दिलचस्प आदमी है। अनीता भी बहुत अच्छी है।

मैं उनको पिछले पन्द्रह सालों से जानता हूं।

क्या आप लोग साथ-साथ पढ़ते थे?

जी हां, हम लोग एक ही कालेज में पढ़ते थे।

बहुत अच्छी बात है। मैं बहुत जल्दी उनसे मिलने की कोशिश करूंगा।

आप मुझे उनका सही पता दीजिये। उनका टेलीफोन नम्बर भी दीजिये।

मैं पहले उनको टेलीफोन करूंगा। फिर उनसे मिलूंगा।

अच्छा, लीजिये उनका पता और टेलीफोन नम्बर। आप जरूर उनसे मिलिये।

पड़ोस में = in the neighborhood		पड़ोसी = neighbor	
अफ़सोस, दुख = regret (sadness)		दिलचस्प = interesting	
दिलचस्पी = interest		सही = correct	
पता = address		जरूर, अवश्य = surely	

III. संख्याएँ 1-50 (Review) :

1-10	एक	दो	तीन	चार	पांच
	छे	सात	आठ	नौ	दस
11-20	ग्यारह	बारह	तेरह	चौदह	पन्द्रह
	सोलह	सत्रह	अठारह	उन्नीस	बीस
21-30	इक्कीस	बाईस	तेईस	चौबीस	पच्चीस
	छब्बीस	सत्ताईस	अड्ढाईस	उनतीस	तीस
31-40	इकतीस	बत्तीस	तैंतीस	चौंतीस	पैंतीस
	छत्तीस	सैंतीस	अड़तीस	उनतालीस	चालीस
41-50	इकतालीस	बयालीस	तैंतालीस	चवालीस	पैंतालीस
	छियालीस	सैंतालीस	अड़तालीस	उनचास	पचास

Lesson - 3

I. Padhiye :

Aazaad Bhaarat

Bhaarat 15 August 1947 ko aazaad huaa.

Uske pahle vo agnrezo(n) kaa gulaam thaa.

Aazaadee ke baad Bhaarat apnee tarakkee ke liye tarah-tarah kee koshishe(n) karne lagaa.

Bhaarat ne krushi, gyaan-vigyaan, vyaapaar, udyog, sikshaa, videsh-sambandh ityaadi kshetro(n) me(n) lagaataar pragati laane kee koshish kee.

Pichhle 56 saalo(n) me(n) Bhaarat ne har kshetra me(n) jo pragati kee hai use dekhkar saaree duniyaa aascharya kartee hai.

Par Bhaarat ke saamne ek badee takleef hai.

Vo uskee badhtee aabaadee hai.

Uskee aabaadee ab ek arab se aage pahu(n)ch gayee hai.

Bhaarat sarkaar use kam karne ke liye tarah-tarah ke prayaas kar rahee hai.

Doosree takleef (samasyaa) asiksha hai.

Ab bhee kayee pradeso(n) me(n) laakho(n) asikshit log hai(n).

Bhaarat sarkaar ne unko sikshit karne ke liye kayee naye naye kadam utthaaye hai(n).

Kashmir kee samasyaa teesree takleef hai.

Sarkaar use suljhaane kee badee koshish kar rahee hai.

Des me(n) shaanti kaayam rakhne kee badee zaroorat hai.

Padosee desho(n) ke saath bhee shaanti kaa sambandh sthaapit karne kee aavashyaktaa hai.

Is ore tarah-tarah kee **koshishe(n) kee jaa rahee hai(n).**

पाठ - 3

I. पढ़िये :

आज़ाद भारत

भारत 15 अगस्त 1947 को आज़ाद हुआ।

उसके पहले वह अंग्रेज़ों का गुलाम था।

आज़ादी के बाद भारत अपनी तरक्की के लिए तरह-तरह की कोशिशें करने लगा।

भारत ने कृषि, ज्ञान-विज्ञान, व्यापार, उद्योग, शिक्षा, विदेश-संबंध इत्यादि क्षेत्रों में लगातार प्रगति लाने की कोशिश की।

पिछले 56 सालों में भारत ने हर क्षेत्र में जो प्रगति की है उसे देखकर सारी दुनिया आश्चर्य करती है।

पर भारत के सामने एक बड़ी तकलीफ़ है।

वह उसकी बढ़ती आबादी है।

उसकी आबादी अब एक अरब से आगे पहुंच गयी है।

भारत सरकार उसे कम करने के लिए तरह-तरह के प्रयास कर रही है।

दूसरी तकलीफ़ (समस्या) अशिक्षा है।

अब भी कई प्रदेशों में लाखों अशिक्षित लोग हैं।

भारत सरकार ने उनको शिक्षित करने के लिए कई नये-नये कदम उठाये हैं।

काश्मीर की समस्या तीसरी तकलीफ़ है।

सरकार उसे सुलझाने की बड़ी कोशिश कर रही है।

देश में शान्ति कायम रखने की बड़ी ज़रूरत है।

पड़ोसी देशों के साथ भी शान्ति का सम्बन्ध स्थापित करने की आवश्यकता है।

इस ओर तरह-तरह की कोशिशें की जा रही हैं।

Naye shabd (New Words)

Aazaad = Independent   Aazaadee* = independence   Gulaam   Slave

Gulaamee* = slavery   Pahle = before/earlier   Baad = after

Tarakkee*, Pragati* = progress   Koshish*/Prayaas = effort

Tarah-Tarah ke = various/different kinds of   Krushi* = agriculture

Gyaan = knowledge   Vigyaan = science   Vyaapaar = trade

Udyog = industry   Şikshaa* = edcuation   Videsh-Sambandh = foreign relation

Ityaadi = etc.   Kshetra = area   Pradesh = region

Lagaataar = continuously   Duniyaa* = world   Pichhlaa × Aglaa = last/previous × next

Takleef* = diffculty   Samasyaa* = problem   Baḍhtee aabaadee* = increasing population

Sarkaar* = Government   Aşikshaa* = illiteracy   Aşikshit = illiterate/uneducated

Laakho(n) = lakhs of   Hazaaro(n) = thousands of   Kadam Uthaa = take steps

Suljhaa = to solve   Shaanti* = peace

Kaayam rakhnaa ⎱
            to establish
Sthaapit karnaa ⎰

zaroorat* / aavashyaktaa* = need / necessity

II. Baathcheeth :

Ab kitne baje hai(n)?   Ab aap kyaa kar rahe hai(n)?

Aapke saath kitne log Hindi seekh rahe hai(n)?

Aap Hindi kakshaa me(n) kab aur kyse aathee hai(n)?

Aap kahaa(n) se aathee hai(n)?

Aap kyo(n) Hindi seekhnaa chaahthee hai(n)?

Kyaa aapke maataa-pitaa Hindi bolthe hai(n)?

Kyaa aapke dost Hindi bolthe hai(n)?

Kyaa aapko kabhee Hindi bolne kaa maukaa milthaa hai?

Kyaa apko Hindi filme(n) dekhne kaa shauk hai?

Aapki kakshaa kitne baje se kitne baje tak chalthee hai?

Aapki kakshaa kitne baje shuroo hothee hai?

Aap kitne baje ghar jaathee hai(n)?

नये शब्द :

आज़ाद	आज़ादी	गुलाम	गुलामी
पहले	बाद	तरक्की / प्रगति	
कोशिश / प्रयास		तरह-तरह के	कृषि
ज्ञान	विज्ञान	व्यापार	उद्योग
शिक्षा	विदेश-संबंध	इत्यादि	क्षेत्र
प्रदेश	लगातार	दुनिया	पिछला अगला
तकलीफ़	समस्या	बढ़ती आबादी	सरकार
अशिक्षा	अशिक्षित	लाखों	हज़ारों
कदम उठा	सुलझा	शान्ति	

कायम रखना / स्थापित करना

ज़रूरत / आवश्यकता

II. बातचीत :

अब कितने बजे हैं?

अब आप क्या कर रहे हैं?

आपके साथ कितने लोग हिन्दी सीख रहे हैं?

आप हिन्दी कक्षा में कब और कैसे आती हैं?

आप कहां से आती हैं?

आप क्यों हिन्दी सीखना चाहती हैं?

क्या आपके माता-पिता हिन्दी बोलते हैं?

क्या आपके दोस्त हिन्दी बोलते हैं?

क्या आपको कभी हिन्दी बोलने का मौका मिलता है?

क्या आपको हिन्दी फ़िल्में देखने का शौक है?

आपकी कक्षा कितने बजे से कितने बजे तक चलती है?

आपकी कक्षा कितने बजे शुरू होती है?

आप कितने बजे घर जाती हैं?

Aap raat kaa bhojan kitne baje karthee hai(n)?

Kyaa aapko Hindi aasaan lagthee hai?

Aap roz kitnaa samay Hindi me(n) sochthee hai(n)?

Kyaa ye(h) ho sakta hai ki aap roz kam-se-kam aadhaa ghantaa Hindi ke liye alag rakhe(n)?

Dhanyavaad.

Maukaa = opportunity

Shauk = interest

Kyaa ye(h) ho sakta hai ki = is it possible that

Samay = time

Soch = to think

Kam-se-kam = at least

Alag rakh = to keep separate

आप रात का भोजन कितने बजे करती हैं?

क्या आपको हिन्दी आसान लगती है?

आप रोज़ कितना समय हिन्दी में सोचती हैं?

क्या यह हो सकता है कि आप रोज़ कम-से-कम आधा घंटा हिन्दी के लिए अलग रखें?

धन्यवाद।

मौका = opportunity

शौक = interest

क्या यह हो सकता है कि = is it possible that

समय = time

सोच = to think

कम से कम = at least

अलग रख = to keep separate

Lesson - 4

I. Paḍhiye :

Bageechaa

Ye(h) gulaabo(n) ka bageechaaa hai.

Yahaa(n) tarah-tarah ke rango(n) ke gulaab hai(n) - Laal, Peele, Bhoore aur safed.

Inkee paththiyaa(n) haree hai(n).

Gulaab sundar hai(n) aur khushboodaar bhee.

Mujhe gulaab ke phool bahut pasand hai(n).

Maalee bageeche ko sa(n)bhaaltaa hai. Peḍo(n) aur paudho(n) ko paanee detha hai aur saare bageeche ko baḍee mehnat se saaf-suthraa rakhthaa hai.

Vo baḍaa hoshiyaar aur mehnatee hai.

Vo bahut eemaandaar bhee hai.

Uskee patnee bhee uske saath bageeche me(n) kaam karthee hai.

Maalee apne bachcho(n) ko khoob paḍhaanaa-likhaanaa chaahtha hai.

Uske teen bachche hai(n) - Do laḍkiyaa(n) aur ek laḍkaa.

Ve teeno(n) bachche hoshiyaar hai(n) aur kabhee-kabhee apne maa(n)-baap kee sahaaytaa bhee karthe hai(n).

Bageeche me(n) aam, santare, kele aur naariyal ke bhee peḍ hai(n).

Aajkal naariyal bahut maha(n)ge hai(n).

Phal aur sabziyaa(n) bhee maha(n)gee hai(n).

Bolo, tumko kaun-sa phal pasand hai?

Mujhe sab phal pasand hai(n); khaaskar aam bahut pasand hai.

Lekin phal meettaa honaa chaahiye.

Aao, hum thoḍaa bageeche me(n) ghoom aaye(n).

पाठ - 4

I. पढ़िये :

बगीचा

यह गुलाबों का बगीचा है।

यहां तरह-तरह के रंगों के गुलाब हैं—लाल, पीले, भूरे और सफेद।

इनकी पत्तियां हरी हैं।

गुलाब सुन्दर हैं और खुशबूदार भी।

मुझे गुलाब के फूल बहुत पसन्द हैं।

माली बगीचे को संभालता है। पेड़ों और पौधों को पानी देता है और सारे बगीचे को बड़ी मेहनत से साफ-सुथरा रखता है।

वह बड़ा होशियार और मेहनती है।

वह बहुत ईमानदार भी है।

उसकी पत्नी भी उसके साथ बगीचे में काम करती है।

माली अपने बच्चों को खूब पढ़ाना-लिखाना चाहता है।

उसके तीन बच्चे हैं—दो लड़कियां और एक लड़का।

वे तीनों बच्चे होशियार हैं और कभी-कभी अपने मां-बाप की सहायता भी करते हैं।

बगीचे में आम, संतरे, केले और नारियल के भी पेड़ हैं।

आजकल नारियल बहुत महंगे हैं।

फल और सब्जियां भी महंगी हैं।

बोलो, तुमको कौन-सा फल पसन्द है?

मुझे सब फल पसन्द हैं; खासकर आम बहुत पसन्द है।

लेकिन फल मीठा होना चाहिए।

आओ, हम थोड़ा बगीचे में घूम आयें।

Naye Shabd (New Words)

Gulaab = rose

Paththee* = leaf (small)

Sa(m)bhaal = to take care of/to manage

Mehanatee = industrious/hardworking

Rakh = to keep, to put   Hoshiyaar = smart/clever

Eemaandaar = faithful, honest

Naariyal = coconut

Mahanga = expensive   Sastaa = cheap

Ghoom = to go round/wander

Bageechaa = garden

Khushboodaar = fragrant

Bhooraa = brown

Maalee = gardener

Mehnat* = labor

Saaf-Suthraa = clean/neat

Sahaaytaa*, madad* = help

Patnee, Beebee* = wife

II. Şareer ke Ang (Parts of body) :

Baal = hair   Sir = head   Maathaa = forehead   Naak* = nose

Kaan = ear   Aa(n)kh* = eye   Mu(n)h = mouth   Chehraa = face

Gardan* = neck   Galaa = throat   Jeebh* = tongue   Daa(n)th = tooth

Ott/Ho(n)tt = lip   Haath = hand   Baa(n)h = arm   Gaal = cheek

Chibuk* = chin   Kohnee* = elbow   U(n)lgee* = finger   Pyr = foot/leg

Naakhoon = finger-nail   Kamar* = waist   Kalaayee* = wrist

Ghutnaa = knee   Putlee* = eyeball   Bhau(n)* = eyebrow   Palak* = eyelashes

Pet = stomach   Peett* = back   Khoon = blood   Dimaag = brain

Dil/Hruday = heart   Phephdaa = lung

नये शब्द :

गुलाब = rose   बगीचा = garden   भूरा = brown

पत्ती = leaf (small)   खुशबूदार = fragrant   माली = gardener

संभाल = to take care of/to manage   मेहनत = labor

मेहनती = industrious/hardworking   साफ-सुथरा = clean/neat

रख = to keep, to put   होशियार = smart/clever   सहायता, मदद = help

ईमानदार = faithful, honest   पत्नी, बीबी = wife   नारियल = coconut

महंगा = expensive   सस्ता = cheap

घूम = to go round/wander

II. शरीर के अंग (Parts of Body) :

बाल = hair	सिर = head	माथा = forehead	नाक* = nose
कान = ear	आंख* = eye	मुंह = mouth	चेहरा = face
गरदन* = neck	गला = throat	जीभ* = tongue	दांत = tooth
ओठ/होंठ = lip	हाथ = hand	बांह = arm	गाल = cheek
चिबुक* = chin	कोहनी* = elbow	उंगली* = finger	पैर = foot/leg
नाखून = fingar-nail	कमर* = waist	कलाई* = wrist	घुटना = knee
पुतली* = eyeball	भौं* = eyebrow	पलक* = eyelashes	पेट = stomach
पीठ* = back	खून = blood	दिमाग = brain	दिल, हृदय = heart
फेफड़ा = lung			

Lesson - 5

I. Paḍhiye :

Kaaryaalay ke Baare me(n)

Hum log New Jersey me(n) rahthe hai(n).

Humaaraa daftar New York me(n) hai.

Hum log kabhee bus se, kabhee rel gaaḍee se aur kabhee motor gaaḍee se New York aathe hai(n).

Is yaatraa me(n) aam taur par ek yaa deḍh ghantaa lag jaathaa hai.

Humaaraa daftar nau baje se paa(n)ch baje tak hai.

Lekin kabhee-kabhee bahut der tak - raat ke das baje tak kaam karnaa paḍthaa hai.

Is daftar me(n) Pachaas log kaam karthe hai(n).

Jab ve log paa(n)ch baje ke baad kaam karthe hai(n) tab unko zyaadaa vethan milthaa hai.

Humaare kaaryaalay me(n) jo log kaam karthe hai(n) ve alag-alag bhaashaaye(n) bolthe hai(n).

Kyo(n)ki yahaa(n) alag-alag desho(n) ke log kaam karthe hai(n),

lekin unki aam bhaasha angrezee hai.

Yahaa(n) sab log ek parivaar kee tarah baḍe pyaar se rahthe hai(n), mil-julkar kaam karthe hai(n).

Ve log aapas me(n) yek doosre ki sahaaytaa bhee karthe hai(n).

Humaare makaan me(n) bees manzile(n) hai(n).

Humaaraa kaaryaalay dasvee(n) manzail par hai.

Yahaa(n) kaam karnevaale log bahut paḍhe-likhe aur hoshiyaar hai(n)

Ve sab kaaryaalay kee tarakkee ke liye bahut kaam karthe hai(n).

Kyonki unko maaloom hai kee kaaryaalay ki tarakkee me(n) hee unki pragati hai.

पाठ - 5

I. पढ़िये :

कार्यालय के बारे में

हम लोग न्यू जर्सी में रहते हैं।

हमारा दफ़्तर न्यूयार्क में है।

हम लोग कभी बस से, कभी रेलगाड़ी से और कभी मोटर गाड़ी से न्यूयार्क आते हैं।

इस यात्रा में आम तौर पर एक या डेढ़ घंटा लग जाता है।

हमारा दफ़्तर नौ बजे से पांच बजे तक है।

लेकिन कभी-कभी बहुत देर तक—रात के दस बजे तक—काम करना पड़ता है।

इस दफ़्तर में पचास लोग काम करते हैं।

जब वे लोग पांच बजे के बाद काम करते हैं तब उनको ज़्यादा वेतन मिलता है।

हमारे कार्यालय में जो लोग काम करते हैं वे अलग-अलग भाषाएँ बोलते हैं।

क्योंकि यहां अलग-अलग देशों के लोग काम करते हैं,

लेकिन उनकी आम भाषा अंग्रेजी है।

यहां सब लोग एक परिवार की तरह बड़े प्यार से रहते हैं, मिल-जुलकर काम करते हैं।

वे लोग आपस में एक-दूसरे की सहायता भी करते हैं।

हमारे मकान में बीस मंज़िलें हैं।

हमारा कार्यालय दसवीं मंज़िल पर है।

यहां काम करनेवाले लोग बहुत पढ़े-लिखे और होशियार हैं।

वे सब कार्यालय की तरक्की के लिए बहुत काम करते हैं।

क्योंकि उनको मालूम है कि कार्यालय की तरक्की में ही उनकी प्रगति है।

Naye Shabd (New Words) :

Kaaryaalay, Daftar = office   Yaatraa*, safar = journey/travel

Aam taur par = generally   Khaaskar = especially

Ek ghantaa lag jaathaa hai = it takes one hour.

Samay = time   Bahut der tak = for a long time (Der is generally
  used for 'delay' or 'delayed time': Also it indicates 'duration'.)

Kaam karnaa paḍthaa hai = has/have to do work.

Pachaas = 50   Vethan = salary   Alag-Alag = different

Aam = general, Mango   Parivaar = family   Pyaar = love

Mil-Julkar kaam karthe hain(n) = (They) work together / unitedly

Aapas me(n) = among themselves / ourselves / yourselves

Manzil* = floor/destination   Hoshiyaar = clever / smart

Unko maaloom hai ki = They know that   Tarakkee*, Pragati* = progress

II. Paṣu-Pakshee (animals - birds) :

Bhaaloo = bear   Bhai(n)saa(m), Bhains(f) = buffalo   Byl = bullock/bull

Gaai* = cow   Oont = camel   Hiran = deer

Bachḍaa = calf   Gadhaa = donkey   Lomḍee = fox

Bakree* = goat   Bandar = monkey   Choohaa = mouse

Sher = lion   Baagh = tiger   Gilharee* = squirrel

Memnaa = lamb   Kauaa/Kauvaa = crow   Koyal* = cuckoo

Murgee* = hen   Ulloo = owl   Totaa/Keer = parrot

Gauraiyaa = sparrow   Giddh = vulture   Bheḍiyaa = wolf

Mor = peacock   Kabootar = pigeon

नये शब्द :

कार्यालय, दफ्तर = office

यात्रा*, सफर = journey/travel

आम तौर पर = generally

खासकर = especially

एक घंटा लग जाता है = it takes one hour.

समय = time

बहुत देर तक = for a long time (देर is generally used for 'delay' or 'delayed time': Also it indicates 'duration'.)

काम करना पड़ता है = has/have to do work.

पचास = 50

वेतन = salary

अलग-अलग = different

आम = general, Mango

परिवार = family

प्यार = love

मिल-जुलकर काम करते हैं = (They) work together / unitedly

आपस में = among themselves / ourselves / yourselves

मंज़िल* = floor/destination

होशियार = clever / smart

उनको मालूम है कि = They know that

तरक्की*, प्रगति* = progress

II. पशु-पक्षी (animals-birds) :

भालू = bear	भैंसा(m), भैंस(f) = buffalo	बैल = bullock/bull
गाय* = cow	ऊंट = camel	हिरन = deer
बछड़ा = calf	गधा = donkey	लोमड़ी = fox
बकरी* = goat	बंदर = monkey	चूहा = mouse
शेर = lion	बाघ = tiger	गिलहरी* = squirrel
मेमना = lamb	कौआ/कौवा = crow	कोयल* = cuckoo
मुर्गी* = hen	उल्लू = owl	तोता/कीर = parrot
गौरेया = sparrow	गिद्ध = vulture	भेड़िया = wolf
मोर = peacock	कबूतर = pigeon	

Lesson - 6

I. Paḍhiye :

Gaa(n)v ka Jeevan

Ye(h) mera gaa(n)v hai. Mera gaa(n)v bahut sundar hai.

Yahaa(n) humaaraa saaraa parivaar rahthaa hai.

Humaare parivaar ke das sadasya hai(n) - Daadaa, Daadee, maa(n), baap, buaa, teen behne(n) aur hum do bhaayee.

Gaa(n)v ka jeevan bahut achchhaa hai. Kyonki yahaa(n) logo(n) kee bheeḍ-bhaaḍ nahee(n) rahthee. Yahaa(n) kee hawaa aur paanee saaf hai(n). Yahaa(n) pradooshan nahee(n) hai. Yahaa(n) kee aabo-hawaa achchhee rahthee hai.

Har mausam me(n) tarah-tarah ke phal-phool milthe hai(n). Taazee sabziyaa(n) yahaa(n) kee khoobee hai.

Yahaa(n) ke log mil-julkar rahthe hai(n) aur apnaa-apnaa kaam karthe hai(n). zyaadaatar log kisaan hai(n). Ve kheto(n) me(n) kaam karthe hai(n) aur anaaj pydaa karthe hai(n). Yahaa(n) chaaval, gehoo(n), gannaa aur makayee pydaa hothe hai(n). Gaa(n)v ke ye anaaj sahro(n) me(n) bikthe hai(n). Ṣahar ke log gaa(n)v kee pydaavaar par nirbhar rahthe hai(n).

Humaare gaa(n)v me(n) ek nadee hai. Nadee kaa paanee saaf rahthaa hai. Is nadee kaa paanee gaa(n)v ke logo(n) kee zaroorate(n) pooraa karthaa hai.

Hum log bus, rel gaaḍee yaa motor gaaḍee se ṣahar jaa sakte hai(n).

Gaa(n)v kaa jeevan shaant aur dostaanaa rahthaa hai.

पाठ - 6

I. पढ़िये

गांव का जीवन

यह मेरा गांव है।

मेरा गांव बहुत सुन्दर है।

यहां हमारा सारा परिवार रहता है।

हमारे परिवार के दस सदस्य हैं—दादा, दादी, मां, बाप, बुआ, तीन बहनें और हम दो भाई।

गांव का जीवन बहुत अच्छा है। क्योंकि यहां लोगों की भीड़-भाड़ नहीं रहती। यहां की हवा और पानी साफ हैं। यहां प्रदूषण नहीं है। यहां की आबोहवा अच्छी रहती है।

हर मौसम में तरह-तरह के फल-फूल मिलते है। ताज़ी सब्जियां यहां की खूबी है।

यहां के लोग मिल-जुलकर रहते हैं और अपना-अपना काम करते हैं। ज्यादातर लोग किसान हैं। वे खेतों में काम करते हैं और अनाज पैदा करते हैं। यहां चावल, गेहूं, गन्ना और मकई पैदा होते हैं। गांव के ये अनाज शहरों में बिकते हैं। शहर के लोग गांव की पैदावार पर निर्भर रहते हैं।

हमारे गांव में एक नदी है। नदी का पानी साफ रहता है। इस नदी का पानी गांव के लोगों की जरूरतें पूरा करता है।

हम लोग बस, रेलगाड़ी या मोटर गाड़ी से शहर जा सकते हैं।

गांव का जीवन शान्त और दोस्ताना रहता है।

II. Naye Shabd :

Jeevan, Zindagee* = life   Parivaar = family   Sadasya = member/members

Buaa = aunt (father's sister) Bheed-bhaad* = crowd   Pradooshan = pollution

Aabo-hawaa* = climate   Khoobee* = speciality   Mil-Julkar = unitedly

Zyaadaatar = majority   Anaaj = foodgrain   Chaaval = rice

Gehoo(n) = wheat   Gannaa, Eekh = sugarcane   Makayee* = maize,

Pydaa kar = to produce   Pydaa ho = to grow   Bik = to be sold

Bech = to sell   Pydaavaar* = produce   Shaant = peaceful

Dostaanaa = friendly   Pooraa kar = to complete / to fulfill

III. Sabziyaa(n) / Tarkaariyaa(n) (Vegetables) :

Sem = green beans   Gobhee*, Band Gobhee * = cabbage

Phoolgobhee* = cauliflower   Gaajar = carrot   Dhaniyaa* = coriander

Kakdee*, Kheeraa = cucumber   By(n)gan = egg plant

Bhindee = okra   Nee(m)boo = lemon   Pyaaj = onion

Lahsun = garlic   Matar = peas   Aaloo = potato

Kaddoo = pumpkin   Moolee* = radish   Paalak = spinach

Sakarkand = sweet potato   Tamaatar = tomato   Pudeenaa = mint

II. नये शब्द :

जीवन, ज़िन्दगी* = life	परिवार = family	सदस्य = member/members
बुआ = aunt (father's sister)	भीड़-भाड़* = crowd	प्रदूषण = pollution
आबो-हवा* = climate	खूबी* = speciality	मिल-जुलकर = unitedly
ज़्यादातर = majority	अनाज = foodgrain	चावल = rice
गेहूं = wheat	गन्ना, ईख = sugarcane	मकई* = **maize, corn**
पैदा कर = to produce	पैदा हो = to grow	बिक = to be sold
बेच = to sell	पैदावार* = produce	शान्त = peaceful
दोस्ताना = friendly	पूरा कर = to complete / to fulfill	

III. सब्ज़ियां / तरकारियां (Vegetables) :

सेम = green beans	गोभी*, बन्दगोभी* = cabbage	
फूलगोभी* = cauliflower	गाजर = carrot	धनिया* = coriander
ककड़ी*, खीरा = cucumber	बैंगन = egg plant	भिंडी = okra
नींबू = lemon	प्याज = onion	लहसुन = garlic
मटर = peas	आलू = potato	कद्दू = pumpkin
मूली* = radish	पालक = spinach	शकरकन्द = sweet potato
टमाटर = tomato	पुदीना = mint	

Lesson - 7

I. Paḍhiye:

New York Ṣahar

Ye(h) New York ṣahar hai.

Ye(h) duniya ke mashhoor ṣaharo(n) me(n) se hai.

Ise chhotee duniya kahaa jaathaa hai.

Kyo(n)ki yahaa(n) duniya ke sab desho(n) ke log rahthe hai(n).

e apnee-apnee bhaashaaye(n) bolthe hai(n). Unkee apnee apnee sanskriti hai. Unkee rahan-sahan khaan-paan aur vesh-bhooshaa alag-alag hai(n).

Har desh ke log apne bachcho(n) ko apnee sanskriti ke baare me(n) sikhaathe hai(n).

Unke apne-apne mandir hai(n); jaise Hindu Mandir, Masjid, Girjaa ghar, Gurudwaaraa, vagairah.

Unko apne-apne dharma kaa paalan karne kee aazaadee hai.

Saal me(n) ek baar har desh ke log apne-apne desh kaa pared nikaalthe hai(n).

Hazaaro(n) log un paredo(n) me(n) ikatte hothe hai(n).

Kyaa tumne kabhee koyee pared dekhaa hai?

Jee haa(n), dekhaa hee nahee(n), shaamil bhee huaa hoo(n).

Itnaa farak hone ke baavjood sab log yahaa(n) pyaar aur dostee ke saath rahthe hai(n).

Ye(h) kahaa jaathaa hai ki ye(h) ṣahar kabhee nahee(n) sotaa hai. Yahaa(n) kuchh-na-kuchh hothaa rahthaa hai.

Yahaa(n) sab tarah kee suvidhaaye(n) hai(n).

Mujhe ye(h) ṣahar bahut pasand hai.

Ye(h) New York ṣahar hai.

पाठ - 7

I. पढ़िये

न्यूयार्क शहर

यह न्यूयार्क शहर है।

यह दुनिया के मशहूर शहरों में से है।

इसे छोटी दुनिया कहा जाता है।

क्योंकि यहां दुनिया के सब देशों के लोग रहते हैं।

वे अपनी अपनी भाषाएँ बोलते हैं। उनकी अपनी-अपनी संस्कृति है। उनकी रहन-सहन, खान-पान और वेश-भूषा अलग-अलग हैं।

हर देश के लोग अपने बच्चों को अपनी संस्कृति के बारे में सिखाते हैं।

उनके अपने अपने मंदिर हैं; जैसे हिन्दू मन्दिर, मसजिद, गिरजा घर, गुरुद्वारा वगैरह।

उनको अपने-अपने धर्म का पालन करने की आज़ादी है।

साल में एक बार हर देश के लोग अपने-अपने देश का परेड निकालते हैं।

हज़ारों लोग उन परेडों में इकट्ठे होते हैं।

क्या तुमने कभी कोई परेड देखा है?

जी हां, देखा ही नहीं, शामिल भी हुआ हूं।

इतना फ़रक होने के बावजूद सब लोग यहां प्यार और दोस्ती के साथ रहते हैं।

यह कहा जाता है कि यह शहर कभी नहीं सोता है। यहां कुछ-न-कुछ होता रहता है।

यहां सब तरह की सुविधाएं हैं।

मुझे यह शहर बहुत पसन्द है।

यह न्यूयार्क शहर है।

II. Naye Shabd :

Mashhoor, Prasiddha = famous

Rahan-Sahan* = pattern of life

Masjid* = Mosque

Gurudwaaraa = Sikh Temple

Aazaadee* = freedom / independence

Shaamil ho = to participate

Ke baavjood = in spite of

Nikaal = to take out

Kuch-na-Kuch = something or the other

Suvidhaa* = facility

Sanskriti* = culture

Vesh-Bhooshaa* = dress

Girjaa Ghar = Church

Vagairah, Aadi, Ityaadi = etcetera

Ikattaa ho = to gather

Farak = difference/s

Dostee* = friendship

Kahaa jaataa hai = is said

Hota rahtaa hai = goes on happening

Sab tarah ka = all kinds of

III. Khaane kee cheeze(n) (Eatables) :

Chaaval = rice

Makayee* = corn/maize

Chhaachh = butter milk

Namak = salt

Kaajoo = cashew nut

Daal* = lentil

Mevaa = dry fruit

Andaa = egg

Rotee*/Chapaatee* = bread

Doodh = milk

Ghee = clarified butter

Cheenee*/Shakkar = sugar

Baadaam = almond

Naariyal = coconut

Tel = oil

Machhlee* = fish

Gehoo(n) = wheat

Makkhan = butter

Paneer = cottage cheese

Gud = jaggery

Chanaa = gram

Khopraa = coconut (dry)

Achaar = pickle

Maa(n)s = meat

II. नये शब्द :

मशहूर, प्रसिद्ध = famous

रहन-सहन* = pattern of life

मसजिद* = Mosque

गुरुद्वारा = Sikh Temple

आज़ादी* = freedom / independence

शामिल हो = to participate

के बावजूद = in spite of

निकाल = to take out

कुछ-न-कुछ = something or the other

सुविधा* = facility

संस्कृति* = culture

वेश-भूषा* = dress

गिरजा घर = Church

वगैरह, आदि, इत्यादि = etcetera

इकट्ठा हो = to gather

फ़रक = difference/s

दोस्ती* = friendship

कहा जाता है = is said

होता रहता है = goes on happening

सब तरह का = all kinds of

III. खाने की चीज़ें :

चावल = rice	रोटी*/चपाती* = bread	गेहूं = wheat
मकई* = corn/maize	दूध = milk	मक्खन = butter
छाछ = butter milk	घी = clarified butter	पनीर = cottage cheese
नमक = salt	चीनी*/शक्कर = sugar	गुड़ = jaggery
काजू = cashew nut	बादाम = almond	चना = gram
दाल* = lentil	नारियल = coconut	खोपरा = coconut (dry)
मेवा = dry fruit	तेल = oil	अचार = pickle
अंडा = egg	मछली* = fish	मांस = meat

Lesson - 8

I. Paḍhiye aur Samjhiye :

Bhayee, ghar ke darvaaze band hai(n). Unhe(n) khol do.

Apne kamre ke darvaaze band karo; unhe(n) mat kholo.

Kyaa tumhaaraa kamraa khulaa hai? Use kabhee khulaa mat choḍo. Hameshaa band rakho.

Kabhee-kabhee hawaa tez chalthee hai. Lekin aaj garmee (umas) bahut hai.

Pankhaa chalaao. Garmee ke mausam me(n) bahut paanee peenaa chahiye.

Nal se paanee aathaa hai. Nal ka paanee saaf zaroor hai. Phir bhee use garam karke hi peenaa chahiye.

Achchhaa hogaa (behtar hogaa) agar hum hameshaa ublaa huaa paanee tandaa karke piye(n).

My(n) hameṣa apne logo(n) ke saath (ke beech) apnee bhaashaa me(n) bolthaa hoo(n). My(n) chahthaa hoo(n) ki aap bhee apnee bhaashaa bolne kee koshish kare(n). Isme(n) dostee hai, bhaayee chaaraa hai; aapsee ektaa kaa anubhav (ehsaas) hai.

Saḍak par chaaro(n) taraf paththar (kankaḍ) hai(n). Ye(h) pathreelaa raastaa hai.

In paththaro(n) ko (kankaḍo(n) ko) hataaiye aur raastaa saff keejiye.

Raastaa saaf ho taaki chalne me(n) koyee takleef na ho.

II. Naye Shabd :

Khul = to be open   Khol = to open   Band = to be closed

Band kar = to close   Mat choḍo = don't leave   Band rakh = to keep closed

पाठ - 8

I. पढ़िये और समझिये :

भाई, घर के दरवाज़े बन्द हैं। उन्हें खोल दो।

अपने कमरे के दरवाज़े बन्द करो। उन्हें मत खोलो।

क्या तुम्हारा कमरा खुला है? उसे कभी खुला मत छोड़ो। हमेशा बन्द रखो।

कभी-कभी हवा तेज़ चलती है। लेकिन आज गरमी (उमस) बहुत है। पंखा चलाओ। गरमी के मौसम में बहुत पानी पीना चाहिये।

नल से पानी आता है। नल का पानी साफ़ ज़रूर है। फिर भी उसे गरम करके ही पीना चाहिए। अच्छा होगा (बेहतर होगा) अगर हम हमेशा उबला हुआ पानी ठंडा करके पियें।

मैं हमेशा अपने लोगों के साथ (के बीच) अपनी भाषा में बोलता हूं। मैं चाहता हूं कि आप भी अपनी भाषा बोलने की कोशिश करें। इसमें दोस्ती है, भाईचारा है; आपसी एकता का अनुभव (एहसास) है।

सड़क पर चारों तरफ़ पत्थर (कंकड़) हैं। यह पथरीला रास्ता है। इन पत्थरों को (कंकड़ों को) हटाइये और रास्ता साफ़ कीजिये। रास्ता साफ़ हो ताकि चलने में कोई तकलीफ न हो।

II. नये शब्द :

खुल = to be open   खोल = to open   बन्द = to be closed
बन्द कर = to close   मत छोड़ो = don't leave   बन्द रख = to keep closed

Garmee* = heat, warmth   Umas* = humidity   Nal = pipe

Garam karke (ubaalkar) = having boiled   Ubla huaa = boiled

Behtar hogaa = (it) would be better   Bhaayeechaaraa = brotherhood

ektaa* = unity   Anubhav/Ehsaas = feeling

Chaaro(n) taraf = everywhere (on all four sides)   Paththar = stone

Kankaḍ = small stone   Pathreelaa raastaa = road filled with stones (rough road)

Hataa = to remove   Taaki = so that

Koyee takleef na ho = let there be no difficulty

III. 12 Maheene (12 months) : (English)

Janvaree	Farvaree	Maarch	Aprail		Mayee	Joon
July	Agast	Sitambar	Aktoobar (Aktobar)	Navambar	Disambar	

Hafte ke saat din :

Somvaar, Mangalvaar, Budhvaar, Guruvaar (Brihaspativaar), Ṣhukravaar, Shanivaar, Itvaar (Ravivaar)

Numbers (Sankhyaaye(n) 51-80 Review) :

51-60

Ikyaavan	Baavan	Tirpan	Chauvan	Pachpan
Chappan	Satthaavan	Attaavan	Unsatt	Saatt

61-70

Iksatt	Baasatt	Tirsatt	Chau(n)satt	Py(n)satt
Chhiyaasatt	Saḍsatt	Aḍsatt	Unhattar	Sattar

71-80

Ikhattar	Bahattar	Tihattar	Chauhattar	Pachhattar
Chhihattar	Sathattar	Atthattar	Unnaasee	Assee

IV. Seekhiye :

a. My(n) apnaa kaam khud kar saktaa hoo(n). (kar saktee hoo(n))

    Vo doosro(n) kee madad khoob kar saktaa hai (kar saktee hai)

गरमी* = heat, warmth   उमस* = humidity   नल = pipe

गरम करके (उबालकर) = having boiled   उबला हुआ = boiled

बेहतर होगा = (it) would be better   भाईचारा = brotherhood

एकता* = unity   अनुभव (एहसास) = feeling

चारों तरफ = everywhere (on all four sides)   पत्थर = stone

कंकड़ = small stone   पथरीला रास्ता = road filled with stones (rough road)

हटा = to remove   ताकि = so that

कोई तकलीफ न हो = let there be no difficulty

III. 12 महीने (अंग्रेज़ी) :

जनवरी	फ़रवरी	मार्च	अप्रैल		मई	जून
जुलाई	अगस्त	सितम्बर	अक्तूबर (अक्टोबर)		नवम्बर	दिसम्बर

हफ़्ते के सात दिन :

सोमवार, मंगलवार, बुधवार, गुरुवार (बृहस्पतिवार), शुक्रवार, शनिवार, इतवार (रविवार)

संख्याएँ - 51-80 (Review) :

51-60

इक्यावन	बावन	तिरपन	चौवन	पचपन
छप्पन	सत्तावन	अट्ठावन	उनसठ	साठ

61-70

इकसठ	बासठ	तिरसठ	चौंसठ	पैंसठ
छियासठ	सड़सठ	अड़सठ	उनहत्तर	सत्तर

71-80

इकहत्तर	बहत्तर	तिहत्तर	चौहत्तर	पचहत्तर
छिहत्तर	सतहत्तर	अठहत्तर	उन्नासी	अस्सी

IV. सीखिये :

a. मैं अपना काम खुद कर सकता हूं (कर सकती हूं)।

वह दूसरों की मदद खूब कर सकता है (कर सकती है)।

Kyaa aap Hindi me(n) bol sake(n)ge (sakengee)?

Jee nahee(n), my(n) khoob samajh sakoo(n)gaa (sakoo(n)gee); Par bolnaa mushkil hai. Isme(n) samay lagegaa.

Ve log kal Hindi kakshaa me(n) nahee(n) aa sake; Koy(n)ki kal bahut baarish thee aur mausam kharaab thaa.

Mera bhaayee aaj daftar nahee(n) jaa sakaa; kyo(n)ki vo beemaar thaa. Shaayad vo kal jaa sakegaa.

b. Garmee kee chhuttiyo(n) ke liye humaaraa school band ho chukaa hai. Garmee ke baad sitambar maheene me(n) vo phir khulegaa.

Humaare bhaayee dafter se aa chuke.

Meree behan doctoree ke paḍhaayee pooree kar chukee hai.

Bhaarat aazaad ho chukaa hai.

My(n) saaraa ṣahar dekh chukaa hoo(n).

Behan ji, kyaa aap apnaa kaam pooraa kar chukee hai(n)?

Jee nahee(n), my(n) apnaa kaam kal pooraa karoongee.

क्या आप हिन्दी में बोल सकेंगे (बोल सकेंगी)?

जी नहीं, मैं खूब समझ सकूंगा (सकूंगी); पर बोलना मुश्किल है। इसमें समय लगेगा।

वे लोग कल हिन्दी कक्षा में नहीं आ सके, क्योंकि कल बहुत बारिश थी और मौसम खराब था।

मेरा भाई आज दफ़्तर नहीं जा सका; क्योंकि वह बीमार था; शायद वह कल जा सकेगा।

b.   गरमी की छुट्टियों के लिए हमारा स्कूल बन्द हो चुका है। गरमी के बाद सितम्बर महीने में वह फिर खुलेगा।

हमारे भाई दफ़्तर से आ चुके।

मेरी बहन डाक्टरी की पढ़ाई पूरी कर चुकी है।

भारत आज़ाद हो चुका है।

मैं सारा शहर देख चुका हूं।

बहनजी, क्या आप अपना काम पूरा कर चुकी हैं?

जी नहीं, मैं अपना काम कल पूरा करूंगी।

Lesson - 9

I. Paḍhiye aur Samjhiye :

Ye(h) kisaan hai. Kisaan khet me(n) kaam kartha hai.

Kisaan hal yaa machine se khet jot thaa hai.

Vo khet see(n)chtha hai; beej bothaa hai. Is tarah chaaval, gehoon, makayee aadi anaaj pydaa karthaa hai.

Kisaan kee mehnat se sabko bhojan milthaa hai.

Khetee me(n) khaad kee baḍee zaroorat hothee hai.

Kisaan saal me(n) lagbhag aatt maheene khoob mehnat karthaa hai.

Darjee kapḍe seethaa hai. Kapḍe kee silaayee me(n) bahut samay lagthaa hai.

Raaj makaan banaathaa hai. Makaan banaane me(n) eent, cement, lakḍee kee cheeze(n) vagairah zarooree hai(n).

Baḍhayee raaj kee madad karthaa hai. Vo lakḍee kaa kaam karthaa hai.

Mochee joote, chappale(n), vagairah chamḍe kee cheeze(n) banaathaa hai.

Ye sab mazdoor hai(n).

Ye mazdoor samaaj ke mazboot hisse hai(n).

In mazdooro(n) ko unkee mehnat ke mutaabik mazdooree milnee chaahiye.

II. Naye Shabd :

Kisaan = farmer	Khet = farm / agricultural land	hal = plough
Jot = to plough	See(n)ch = to water / irrigate	Beej = seed
Bo = sow	Is tarah = thus / in this manner	Mehnat* = hard work
Bhojan (Khaanaa)= food	Khetee* = farming, cultivation	Khaad* = manure
Lagbhag = about, approximately	Darjee = tailor	See = to stitch
Silaayee* = stitching	Bahut samay lagthaa hai = it takes lot of time	
Raaj = mason, builder	Eent* = brick	Cheez* = thing

पाठ – 9

I. पढ़िये और समझिये :

यह किसान है। किसान खेत में काम करता है।

किसान हल या मशीन से खेत जोतता है।

वह खेत सींचता है; बीज बोता है; इस तरह चावल गेहूं, मकई आदि अनाज पैदा करता है।

किसान की मेहनत से सबको भोजन मिलता है।

खेती में खाद की बड़ी ज़रूरत होती है।

किसान साल में लगभग आठ महीने खूब मेहनत करता है।

दर्जी कपड़े सीता है।

कपड़े की सिलाई में बहुत समय लगता है।

राज मकान बनाता है। मकान बनाने में ईंट, सीमेंट, लकड़ी की चीज़ें वगैरह ज़रूरी हैं।

बढ़ई राज की मदद करता है। वह लकड़ी का काम करता है।

मोची जूते, चप्पलें वगैरह चमड़े की चीज़ें बनाता है।

ये सब मज़दूर हैं।

ये मज़दूर समाज के मज़बूत हिस्से हैं।

इन मज़दूरों को उनकी मेहनत के मुताबिक मज़दूरी मिलनी चाहिये।

II. नये शब्द :

किसान = farmer	खेत = farm / agricultural land	हल = plough
जोत = to plough	सींच = to water / irrigate	बीज = seed
बो = sow	इस तरह = thus / in this manner	मेहनत* = hard work
भोजन (खाना) = food	खेती* = farming, cultivation	खाद* = manure
लगभग = about, approximately	दर्जी = tailor	सी = to stitch
सिलाई* = stitching	बहुत समय लगता है = it takes lot of time	
राज = mason, builder	ईंट* = brick	चीज़* = thing

Baḍhyee = carpenter   Mochee = shoemaker   Jootaa = shoe
Chappal* = slipper, sandal Chamḍaa = leather, skin   Mazdoor = worker/s
Hissaa = part   Ke mutaabik = according to Mazdooree* = wages

III. Makaan ke bhaag (hisse) (parts of building) :

Phaatak = gate   Darvaazaa = door   Farsh/Zameen* = floor
Deevaar* = wall   Khiḍkee* = window   Snaan ghar = bath room
Sone kaa kamra = bed room Chhat* = ceiling / roof
Khaane kaa kamraa = dining room
Byttak khaanaa, Byttne kaa kamraa = drawing room   Mehmaan kaa kamraa = guest room
Paḍhne kaa kamraa = study room   Rasoyee ghar = kitchen

IV. Numbers (Sankhyaaye)(n) (Review) :

81-90

| Ikyaasee | Bayaasee | Tiraasee | Chauraasee | Pachaasee |
| Chhiyaasee | **Satthaasee** | Attaasee | Navaasee | Nabbe |

91-100

| Ikyaanave | Baanave | Tiraanave | Chauraanave | Panchaanave |
| Chhiyaanave | Sathaanave | Attaanave | Ninyaanave | Sau |

बढ़ई = carpenter   मोची = shoemaker   जूता = shoe
चप्पल* = slipper, sandal   चमड़ा = leather, skin   मज़दूर = worker/s
हिस्सा = part   के मुताबिक = according to   मज़दूरी* = wages

III. मकान के भाग (हिस्से) :

फाटक = gate   दरवाज़ा = door   फ़र्श/जमीन* = floor
दीवार* = wall   खिड़की* = window   स्नान घर = bath room
सोने का कमरा = bed room   छत* = ceiling / roof   खाने का कमरा = dining room
बैठक खाना, बैठने का कमरा = **drawing room**   मेहमान का कमरा = guest room
पढ़ने का कमरा = study room   रसोई घर = kitchen

IV. संख्याएँ – 81-100 (Review) :

81-90

इक्यासी	बयासी	तिरासी	चौरासी	पचासी
छियासी	सत्तासी	अड़ासी	नवासी	नब्बे

91-100

इक्यानवे	बानवे	तिरानवे	चौरानवे	पंचानवे
छियानवे	सत्तानवे	अड़ानवे	निन्यानवे	सौ

Lesson - 10

I. Paḍhiye aur Samjhiye :

Meraa bhaayee beemaar hai. Use jukaam aur bukhaar hai.

Vo ilaaj ke liye doctor ke paas jaanevaalaa hai.

Use turant doctor ke paas jaanaa chaahiye.

Doctor uski jaa(n)ch karegaa aur zarooree davaaiyaa(n) degaa.

Davaakhaane me(n) davaaiyaa(n) milengee.

Baraabar davaa khaane aur aaraam karne se meraa bhaayee tteek ho jaayegaa.

My(n) swasth hoo(n). Meraa swaasthya achchhaa hai.

Mujhe saaf-suthree jagah par rahnaa chaahiye.

Mujhe achchhaa aur saaf khaanaa khaanaa chaahiye.

Swasth rahne ke liye saaf havaa aur paanee ki zaroorat hai.

Shareer saaf ho, dil saaf ho, dimaag shant ho, vaataavaran achchhaa ho, tab insaan ka jeevan saphal hogaa.

Aaj saaree duniyaa me(n) himsaa hai - shaanti nahee(n) hai.

Har jagah par - har desh me(n) aam jantaa ko bahut takleefe(n) hai(n).

Achchhaa khaanaa nahee(n) milthaa hai; Paanee kee tangee hai.

Log aapas me(n) dushman kee tarah bartaav karthe hai(n).

Log ek doosre kee madad karnaa bhool gaye hai(n).

Iskaa kaaran swaarth hai.

Log swaarth se door rahe(n); insaan insaan kee sahaaytaa karnaa seekhe.

Aaiye, hum sab is sa(n)saar kee khushhaalee aur shaanti ke liye koshish kare(n).

Jahaa(n) tak ho sake, ek doosre kee madad kare(n) aur sabke saath pyaar aur dostee baante(n).

पाठ - 10

I. पढ़िये और समझिये :

मेरा भाई बीमार है। उसे जुकाम और बुखार है।

वह इलाज के लिए डाक्टर के पास जानेवाला है।

उसे तुरन्त डाक्टर के पास जाना चाहिये।

डाक्टर उसकी जांच करेगा और ज़रूरी दवाइयां देगा।

दवाखाने में दवाइयां मिलेंगी।

बराबर दवा खाने और आराम करने से मेरा भाई ठीक हो जायेगा।

मैं स्वस्थ हूं। मेरा स्वास्थ्य अच्छा है।

मुझे साफ़-सुथरी जगह पर रहना चाहिये।

मुझे अच्छा और साफ़ खाना खाना चाहिये।

स्वस्थ रहने के लिए साफ हवा और पानी की ज़रूरत है।

शरीर साफ हो, दिल साफ़ हो, दिमाग शान्त हो, वातावरण अच्छा हो, तब इनसान का जीवन सफल होगा।

आज सारी दुनिया में हिंसा है—शांति नहीं है।

हर जगह पर—हर देश में आम जनता को बहुत तकलीफें हैं।

अच्छा खाना नहीं मिलता है; पानी की तंगी है।

लोग आपस में दुश्मन की तरह बरताव करते हैं।

लोग एक-दूसरे की मदद करना भूल गये हैं।

इसका कारण स्वार्थ है।

लोग स्वार्थ से दूर रहें; इनसान इनसान की सहायता करना सीखे।

आइये, हम सब इस संसार की खुशहाली और शांति के लिए कोशिश करें।

जहां तक हो सके, एक-दूसरे की मदद करें और सबके साथ प्यार और दोस्ती बांटें।

II. Naye Shabd:

Beemaar = sick   Beemaaree* = sickness   Swasth, Tandurust = healthy

Swaasthya, Tandurustee* = good health   Jukaam = cold

Bukhaar = fever   Ilaaj = treatment   Turant = immediately

Jaa(n)ch* = test   Davaa*, Davaayee* = medicine

Davaakhaanaa = Pharmacy / Hospital   Saaf, Saaf-suthraa = clean

Jagah* = place   Şareer = body   Dil = heart (feelings)

Dimaag = mind / brain   Shaant = peaceful   Shaanti* = peace

Vaataavaran = atmosphere   Insaan = human being   Jeevan = life

Saphal = successful   Samsaar, Duniya* = world   Aam = common

Jantaa* = public   Takleef* = difficulty   Tangee* = scarcity

Dushman = enemy   Bartaav = behaviour   Swaarth = selfishness

Door rah = to be far / to be away   Khushhaalee* = wellbeing / prosperity

Jahaa(n) tak ho sake = as far as possible   Baa(n)t = to share / divide

Dostee* = friendship

Dhanyavaad/Shukriyaa = Thanks

II. नये शब्द :

बीमार = sick   बीमारी* = sickness   स्वस्थ, तन्दुरुस्त = healthy

स्वास्थ्य, तन्दुरुस्ती* = good health   जुकाम = cold

बुखार = fever   इलाज = treatment   तुरन्त = immediately

जांच* = test   दवा*, दवाई* = medicine

दवाखाना = Pharmacy / Hospital   साफ़, साफ़-सुथरा = clean

जगह* = place   शरीर = body   दिल = heart (feelings)

दिमाग = mind / brain   शांत = peaceful   शान्ति* = peace

वातावरण = atmosphere   इनसान = human being   जीवन = life

सफल = successful   संसार, दुनिया* = world   आम = common

जनता* = public   तकलीफ* = difficulty   तंगी* = scarcity

दुश्मन = enemy   बरताव = behaviour   स्वार्थ = selfishness

दूर रह = to be far / to be away   खुशहाली* = wellbeing / prosperity

जहां तक हो सके = as far as possible   बांट = to share / divide

दोस्ती* = friendship

धन्यवाद/शुक्रिया

Microbial Culture And Applications

INTRODUCTION